Women and
Culture Series

The Women and Culture Series is dedicated to books that illuminate the lives, roles, achievements, and status of women, past or present.

Fran Leeper Buss
   La Partera: Story of a Midwife

Valerie Kossew Pichanick
   Harriet Martineau: The Woman and Her Work, 1802-76

Sandra Baxter and Marjorie Lansing
   Women and Politics: The Invisible Majority

Estelle B. Freedman
   Their Sisters' Keepers: Women's Prison Reform in America, 1830-1930

Susan C. Bourque and Kay Barbara Warren
   Women of the Andes: Patriarchy and Social Change in Two Peruvian Towns

Marion S. Goldman
   Gold Diggers and Silver Miners: Prostitution and Social Life on the Comstock Lode

Page duBois
   Centaurs and Amazons: Women and the Pre-History of the Great Chain of Being

PAGE DUBOIS won honorable mention in the Hamilton Prize competition for 1979. The Alice and Edith Hamilton Prize is named for two outstanding women scholars: Alice Hamilton (educated at the University of Michigan Medical School), a pioneer in environmental medicine; and her sister Edith Hamilton, the renowned classicist. The Hamilton Prize competition is supported by the University of Michigan Horace H. Rackham School of Graduate Studies and by private donors.

Camera-ready copy has been provided by the author.

CENTAURS AND AMAZONS

CENTAURS AND AMAZONS

Women and the Pre-History of the Great Chain of Being

Page duBois

ANN ARBOR

THE UNIVERSITY OF MICHIGAN PRESS

Library of Congress Cataloging in Publication Data

DuBois, Page.
  Centaurs and Amazons.

  (Women and culture series)
  Includes bibliographical references and index.
  1. Civilization, Greek. 2. Women—Greece—History.
3. Amazons. 4. Centaurs. 5. Chain of being (Philosophy)
I. Title. II. Series.
DF93.D8   938   82-4821
ISBN 0-472-10021-1   AACR2

For Bob

Preface

This book began as a study of Amazons, the band of fearless, independent creatures so often inspiring to women now, near the end of the twentieth century A.D. Studying the myth of the Amazons in the fifth and fourth centuries B.C., however, I realized that just as a new Amazonian myth belongs to our history of liberation movements, of changes in the sex/gender system, of new ideas of community, so the ancient myth of Amazons is embedded in a network of events, ideas, and social relations. Thus this study became an attempt to see the whole of a complex system, the ancient Athenian speculation about sexual, racial, and species difference, in works of visual as well as verbal art, in myths, vase-paintings, monumental sculpture, tragedy, comedy, philosophy. It is a study of culture, of a particular culture's ideas of same and other; my goal was a mapping of how the changing representation of these patterns of same and other occurred in the world of the Athenians. A deliberate effort was required, to transgress the limits of traditional academic disciplines and to move towards a sense of a complex lived reality.

Thus this book is not "history of ideas," not art history, philosophy or literary criticism. And its writing demanded certain polemical choices. I limited my choice of examples, omitting some significant works of visual art; others were selected because they seemed illustrative of a patterning at work in Greek culture. I did not intend to offer an encyclopedia of all references to difference in the ancient world. Three tragedies, the *Persae*, the *Trachiniae*, and the *Medea*, were chosen because they are masterpieces, because they exemplify principles of reasoning about sameness and otherness. To be exhaustive, to mention every tragedy in which difference is an issue, seemed to me to risk losing the lines of my argument in a mass of detail.

This is a polemical work on a variety of cultural forms and it treats each work as it relates to the problematic in question, not as an isolated artistic phenomenon. The selection of material to serve as the object of study was intentional, to enable discussion of the ideas which interested me. Such polemical choices always run the risk of offending scholars of particular disciplines; I am grateful for advice received from many scholars, and hope to have made a beginning for myself toward breaking down boundaries in classical scholarship, a field which seems to me ideally suited for a more totalizing vision.

This study attempts to reconcile a diachronic with a synchronic analysis. It treats fifth-century ideas of difference as a system, while acknowledging a progress within the fifth century of speculation about difference. It maintains that there is a rupture with analogical discourse in the fourth century, and tries as well to situate this rupture in a continuum. I hope it will be of interest to feminist scholars, to historians and makers of cultural change, as well as to classicists.

Because the change discussed here is so fundamental to the history of Western thought about difference and hierarchy, I have wanted to make the text accessible to the reader who does not read Greek. I have transliterated some Greek words, indicating *omega* and *eta* with the circumflex accent. The transliteration of Greek names varies, since I have in general followed the practice of using the form more familiar to most readers.

Acknowledgments

I want to thank the friends, colleagues, and teachers whose support helped me to write this book: the late Robert C. Elliott, whose generosity was boundless and who is sorely missed, Froma Zeitlin, exemplary scholar and friend, Jean-Pierre Vernant, from whom I have learned so much, Alain Renoir, who taught me the difference between humans and human beings, Marcel Detienne, who read the manuscript with great care and gave illuminating counsel, Carol Becker, dear friend, and Shirley Hecht, Saul Steier, Charles Segal, Susan Kirkpatrick, Andrew Wright, Roy Harvey Pearce, Louis Montrose, Joseph Fontenrose, and most of all, Bob Edelman.

The Committee on Research of the Academic Senate, University of California at San Diego, provided research funds for this study which I gratefully acknowledge; I would also like to thank the University's Office of Graduate Studies and Research for aid in its publication.

I am grateful to Susan Walker, Assistant Keeper of the Department of Greek and Roman Antiquities of the British Museum. The trustees of the British Museum have graciously granted me permission to reproduce photographs of works of art I discuss in the text. Thanks also are due to the librarians of the British Library, of the American School in Athens, of the Ecole Normale Supérieure in Paris, and of the University of California's libraries in La Jolla and in Berkeley.

Finally, my thanks to John Peradotto, who made many helpful comments on the manuscript, and who as editor of *Arethusa* has granted me permission to use parts of two essays, "On Horse/Men, Amazons, and Endogamy," *Arethusa* 12.1 (1979), 35-49, and "On the Invention of Hierarchy," forthcoming.

Contents

Introduction

The transition from predominantly narrative discourse—history, tragedy, and comedy—to the discourse of a new philosophy, a transition which occurs in the fourth century B.C., is one of the most significant shifts in the history of Western culture. It marks, in part, the change from a mythic, literary, poetic consciousness to one which examines problems in terms of *logos*, reason.[1] The most important literary genres of the fourth century are the dialogue, the treatise, and the oration. The end of celebratory ritual art—even Herodotos read his history aloud—is revealed in the content of the later prose texts.[2] They are works concerning the right conduct of life and of the city, yet they are articulated in isolation from the practical debates of the *polis*, the city proper. The philosopher stands aloof from the city and prescribes a structure for it; his discourse is produced for the oligarchy, those "best" for whom problems arise as they attempt to fix the city in an eternal, unchanging pattern.

This study is concerned with describing part of the shift from literary to philosophical discourse, from the ritual production of Aeschylus' dramas made by and for the city, to the discourse of the philosophers Plato and Aristotle, whose project was clearly defined for an audience of the elite. Scholars have in the past considered this shift; such classicists as F.M. Cornford, Eric Havelock, and F. Solmsen illuminate many of its major features.[3] Recently, however, attention has turned away from the period of the transition between fifth and fourth centuries to that marked by the formation of the democratic *polis* of the sixth and fifth centuries. Jean-Pierre Vernant, for example, has shown how mythic thought gives way to legal, rational discourse in the context of the classical city.[4] He describes the progress from "mythic" to rational thought as the process of the city's thinking itself, acting

out, especially in tragic drama, the principles by which the united
and equal citizens of Athens will live together. Vernant shows
how, in the *Antigone*, Sophocles gives play to the tension between
conflicting ideas of *nomos*, law.[5] Tragic form itself is seen to
express the contradiction between the old way and the new, in
that single actors and the chorus represent in various ways the old
"lyric" world and the individualistic potential in the classical city.[6]

Although this work is valuable in is contribution to the study
of the formation of the classical democracy, it is important not to
forget the crucial rupture between the Greek classical city and the
imperial civilization which followed it.[7] The discourse of the
fourth-century philosophers prepared the way for that new world
and in addition posed the questions which remained at the heart
of Western philosophy for centuries. Now once again it is possible and necessary to approach the moment of transition from the
world of that city to the world of Plato and Aristotle, one in which
problems arise which are formulated in new ways, one into which
the figure of Alexander is to intervene and bring on the end of
the *polis*.[8]

My purpose here is to describe an aspect of the rupture
between the literary discourse of the fifth century and the philosophical discourse of the fourth. Beginning with the thinking of
the democratic city of the fifth century, I will end by showing
briefly how it was changed in the time of Plato and Aristotle. I
am concerned with a particular area of speculation, the ideas of
difference—sexual, racial, species difference—in the fifth and
fourth centuries B.C. In the shift from poetic and artistic production to "philosophy," there is a corresponding and, I will argue,
related shift in thinking about these kinds of difference. In general terms, there is a break, a shift from speculation based primarily on polarity and analogy to speculation using a hierarchical
logic. The shift from polarity to hierarchy corresponds to the shift
from the democratic city of the fifth century to a period in the
fourth century of questioning the *polis* as a form. A fundamental
crisis is brought on by the Peloponnesian War of 431-404, by subsequent social conflict within Athens, by returning prosperity and
by a growing dependence on slavery. The new philosophy, as a
hierarchizing, rational form of discourse, is born of these changes.

That polarizing, analogical discourse is often characteristic of fifth-century speculation about difference is one of the contentions of this study. The object of analysis is not any particular institution, nor is it the gradual or abrupt appearance of a new science. It is rather a system of utterances about the notion of difference, phrased in terms of the individual's existence and in terms of the society of the Greeks as a whole. This analysis of the pattern of polarizing and analogical reasoning concerning difference, a characteristic of the more literary production of fifth-century thinkers, owes much to the work of G.E.R. Lloyd on ancient modes of thinking. He describes the processes I am alluding to thus:

> Two types of category oversimplification seem to be particularly common in early Greek argumentation. (1) Opposites of any type tend to be taken as mutually exclusive and exhaustive alternatives [i.e. polarity] . . . (2) The relationship of similarity tends to be assimilated to that of complete identity [i.e. analogy]. . . .[9]

The work of Lloyd is richly detailed; he catalogues many uses of polarity and analogy, particularly in the work of the pre-Socratics. In their cosmological and biological speculation, they used polarity and analogy constantly. In archaic cosmological theory, for example, the cosmic order is likened to a social or political order, to a living being, or to the product of "intelligent, designing agencies."[10]

Lloyd suggests a shift from a prephilosophical to a philosophical world, even though he is working primarily with what I would consider philosophical texts, the works of the pre-Socratics.[11] I am concerned with works of the same period, but with the literary texts rather than with those of these philosophers, in part because his work is exhaustive, in part because political and social discourse about difference among living beings is created in the public literary art of the *polis*. The object of this study is less the development of logic, or the emergence of philosophy from a "prephilosophical" era, than it is what A.O. Lovejoy called "dialectical motives":

You may, namely, find much of the thinking of an individual, a school, or even a generation, dominated and determined by one or another turn of reasoning, trick of logic,
methodological assumption, which if explicit would amount
to a large and important and perhaps highly debatable proposition in logic or metaphysics.[12]

The historians, tragedians, philosophers of the fifth century B.C.
often thought in the characteristic "dialectical motives" of polarity
and analogy, and their discourse turns on such logic.

Speculation about difference is a subcategory of the thinking
and literary production of the fifth century, and as such it reveals
the characteristic "dialectical motive." In the fifth century, the
earliest formulations about difference establish a series of polarities which are linked by analogy. That is, the definition of the
norm, the human subject, proceeds through a catalogue of
difference. The human Greek male, the subject of history and of
the culture of the *polis*, is defined in relation to a series of
creatures defined as different. He is at first simply not-animal,
not-barbarian, not-female:

Greek/barbarian
Male/female
Human/animal

The sum of these polarities yields the norm, the Greek male
human being, and the others, on the opposite side of the series of
polarities, are grouped together by analogy. Barbarian is like
female is like animal; these "different" beings share attributes
and function essentially to define the norm through opposition.

In subsequent elaboration of the speculative process, the
playwrights and artists of the fifth century began to focus more
directly on the subject of *polis* culture, the Greek male human
being. In considering him as the center of culture, they moved
away from the polarizing logic of the earlier period to a model
focusing on the citizen, and on his relations with his equals, the
isonomoi of the city. The other—alien, female, bestial—is
excluded, in this discourse, from culture and set at the boundaries
of the city to define it as a circle of equals:

animal

barbarian   Greek male human = Greek male human

female

In literary discourse, the metaphor of marriage, as a founding and sustaining act of culture, was set against that of war, *polemos.* Equals were to exchange women: those outside the circle existed in an agonistic relationship to the body of citizens.

In this model of the city, however, the position of women was gradually revealed as contradictory, since women were the objects of the culture-founding act of exchange. They were excluded from the city yet necessary for its reproduction. They came to represent a potentially dangerous, even poisonous force which was both within the city and outside it.

With the eruption of the Peloponnesian War, the impossibilities of sustaining a polarizing and analogical view of difference became clear. The vocabulary of difference no longer reflected the logic of reality. Those outside the city were revealed to have broken in—Greek warred with Greek, man with woman. The Greek male human struggled against imaginary barbarism, bestiality, and effeminization. The outside had invaded, and the city was threatened in its very idea of itself. In tragedy and in works of art the categories of differentiation through analogy were exposed as inadequate. The result was a rupture, a new ordering of social relations based not on polarity and analogy but rather on hierarchy—within the individual, within the city, within the cosmos as a whole. It is this reordering, this new logic, which is the project of the philosophers Plato and Aristotle and which established the "great chain of being," whose links are forged in relations of superiority and subordination.

When discussing difference, I mean the ways in which a subject, a person who uses language, defines himself and his own kind in terms of 'same' and 'other.' This idea of difference is different from that of Jacques Derrida whose work on the subject has recently been so influential. He defines the infinitive *différer*, from which he derives *différance*, in the following manner:

On the one hand, it indicates difference as distinction, inequality, or discernibility; on the other, it expresses the inter-
position of delay, the interval of a *spacing* and *temporalizing*
that puts off until 'later' what is presently denied, the possible that is presently impossible. . . . In the one case "to
differ" signified nonidentity; in the other case it signifies the
order of the *same.*[13]

Derrida's emphasis on the temporal dimension of the concept of
difference attempts to undo the very notions of presence and subject. I, on the other hand, seek here to treat the way in which the
Greek subject situated himself ideologically in his present.

In focusing on the question of difference, as a logical and
social issue, this study examines a concern internal to Greek civilization. The question is, for the Greeks, related to ideas of marriage, endogamy, and war, to the city and what lies outside it. My
inquiry begins with the utterance of an individual. In his *Lives of
Eminent Philosophers*, Diogenes Laertius recounts this anecdote
about Thales:

Hermippus in his *Lives* refers to Thales the story which is
told by some of Socrates, namely, that he used to say there
were three blessings for which he was grateful to Fortune:
"first, that I was born a human being and not one of the
brutes; next, that I was born a man and not a woman;
thirdly, a Greek and not a barbarian." ("*prôton men hoti
anthrôpos egenomên kai ou thêrion, eita hoti anêr kai ou gunê,
triton hoti Hellên kai ou barbaros.*")[14]

[1.33]

Thales' statement, although not reported until long after his
death, establishes the terms of this study, the elements by which
the definition of man was expressed through analogy. The
speaker, clearly superior to the kinds of being he enumerates, de-
limits the range of knowable beings. The "others" are related to
each other by their otherness, through analogy. He defines himself in terms of difference from them, and situates himself in a
universe of animate beings as human, male, Greek, like all those
so named.

He does not thank fortune that he is not a god. Although the question of difference between gods and men is a crucial one for the culture of antiquity, it is not strictly relevant to the subject of this study. I am concerned with differentiation of kinds among living creatures on earth, in the earliest versions of anthropology, and thus the question of immortality assumes a lesser importance. Clearly the difficulty of human existence and its finitude are at the heart of much tragic drama. But in a sense the possibility of immortality is set aside as the city comes into being. The difference between gods and men is put in abeyance and what is immediately at issue is the quality of their relationship. How are men to know the gods? How are they to conduct their lives on earth in light of the gods' existence?

The case of Pindar is important here, since he illustrates an earlier stage in the development of Greek thinking. Pindar is most concerned not with relations among men, as are the tragedians, but with the connections between men and the gods. Thus, although his poetry is contemporary with the plays of Aeschylus, he belongs to another, more archaic world. John Finley has shown how the two, Pindar and Aeschylus, share a mode of thought which he terms "symbolic"; Finley's study of the two brilliantly delineates their shared ways of thinking.[15] Yet he agrees in essence with the judgement of Eduard Meyer that Pindar is a spokesman of a dying, Aeschylus of a growing culture.[16] Pindar is concerned with oligarchic, aristocratic culture, with the rare victor, the king, the poet, the extraordinary man who comes to terms with his own mortality and for an instant breaks into contact with the gods.

In the myth of Prometheus and Zeus, Hesiod had described a time before the division between gods and men, before their estrangement and before the existence of women.[17] Thereafter, the possibility of such community is lost; attention in Greek tragedy shifts toward a life on earth, among mortals, a life which is consistent with the will of the gods.

Classicists have not considered fully the question of difference, although certain scholars have focused on aspects of the problem. A volume of the Fondation Hardt series considered Greeks and barbarians.[18] The work of H.C. Baldry, *The Unity of Mankind in Greek Thought*, is another important study in this area, although he focuses attention primarily on the gradual emergence of an idealistic union of all peoples. I would rather stress the tightening of categories of difference in the fourth century.[19]

Other classicists have contributed important studies to the history of Greek culture, without considering the issue of difference as such. Eric Havelock, in *The Liberal Temper in Greek Politics*, has carefully delineated the beginnings in the fifth century of liberal opposition to conservative thought.[20] Thomas Cole's *Democritus and the Sources of Greek Anthropology* also traces the threads of a historical and developmental attitude toward human culture among the Greeks.[21] Other classicists have considered the progression of literary and philosophical discourse, notably Bruno Snell in his history of Greek thought, *The Discovery of the Mind*.[22] John Finley also has lucidly discussed the evolution of Greek consciousness, both in *Pindar and Aeschylus*, and in his *Four Stages of Greek Thought*.[23]

In the field of cultural history, the work of the French classicists J.-P. Vernant, *Les origines de la pensée grecque*, and Marcel Detienne, especially *Les maîtres de vérité en Grèce archaïque*[24] are extremely valuable texts. Yet they focus on an earlier period than that which concerns me here. In their most recent research, both Vernant and Detienne have been engaged in work on the synchronic whole of Greek culture.[25] The fascinating *Jardins d'Adonis*, for example, delineates an elaborate system of codes which defined Greek thinking about marriage, cooking, astrology. Detienne's superb essay is concerned with a totality rather than with changes in patterns of thinking over time.[26] René Girard's major study of Greek tragedy, *La violence et le sacré*, is illuminating in its discussion of sacrifice and difference, but its emphasis is on the universal problem of what Girard calls "la crise sacrificielle" and, as will become clear, our views on hierarchy differ radically.[27]

In general, historians of social thought and historians of philosophy have neglected the global significance of the patterns they identify, and their workings in ancient culture as a whole. None of these scholars touches on the problem of difference as such in fifth- and fourth-century culture, in art and literature as well as in philosophical and scientific texts. The most specifically relevant historical work deals with the institution of slavery in ancient

Greece. Robert Schlaifer, G.R. Morrow, M. Finley and others have made important contributions to the study of slavery.[28] Significant research is now being done in Germany by Joseph Vogt and others on slavery as a cultural as well as an historical phenomenon.[29] Yet none of these works is focused directly on the general notion of difference in social life, on sexual and species as well as racial difference.

This question is important in part because of the influence of Greek philosophy on all subsequent Western philosophy. Hierarchical ideas of difference formulated by Plato and Aristotle continue to define relations of dominance and submission in Western culture and in philosophical discourse today. It is essential to understand the context in which the work of Plato and Aristotle was created, to see it as a response to social conditions and to a historical process as well as an attempt to reason about the world. Historians of the Western intellectual tradition tend to ignore what preceded Plato and Aristotle, to define these philosophers' formulations as Urtexts which give innocent expression to certain problematics which remain at the heart of Western philosophy.

I am interested in particular in A.O. Lovejoy's seminal work, *The Great Chain of Being.* Lovejoy traces a particular version of hierarchy throughout Western thought, beginning with Plato. In his preface, Lovejoy remarks that the great chain of being "has been one of the half-dozen most potent and persistent presuppositions in Western thought" (vii). The history of the great chain begins with Plato, whose Idea of the Good, or god, is the source of all lesser creatures derived from it. Plato's concept of "a Self-Transcending Fecundity" was the source of the "temporal and material and extremely multiple and variegated universe" (49). Plato also, according to Lovejoy, established the "principle of plenitude," the notion that "no genuine potentiality of being can remain unfulfilled . . ." (52). Aristotle added to the idea of the fullness of the universe the principle of continuity: "If there is between two given natural species a theoretically possible intermediate type, that type must be realized—and so on *ad indefinitum . . .*" (58). And . . . "it was he who chiefly suggested to naturalists and philosophers of later times the idea of arranging (at least) all animals in a single graded *scala naturae* according to their degree of 'perfection' " (58). Lovejoy adds to these principles a third, "the principle of unilinear gradation" (59), that is, the notion that all things could be ranked in a single order, according to their degree of privation. The result of the thinking of the Greek philosophers was, according to Lovejoy:

> . . . the conception of the universe as a "Great Chain of Being," composed of an immense, or—by the strict but seldom rigorously applied logic of the principle of continuity—of an infinite, number of links ranging in hierarchical order from the meagerest kind of existents, which barely escape non-existence, through "every possible" grade up to the *ens perfectissimum*—or, in a somewhat more orthodox version, to the highest possible kind of creature, between which and the Absolute Being the disparity was assumed to be infinite—every one of them differing from that immediately above and that immediately below it by the "least possible" degree of difference.
>
> [p. 59]

Lovejoy traces this "unit-idea" through Western thought, subtly analyzing the contradictions, the fusions and fissions of the principles which compose it. In a very brief discussion of the social consequences of the great chain in the eighteenth century (206-7), Lovejoy cites Soame Jenyns: "The universe resembles a large and well-regulated family, in which all the officers and servants, and even the domestic animals, are subservient to each other in a proper subordination" (207). Only here does Lovejoy consider the ways in which the idea of the chain could be used to justify a hierarchicized world, a world of unchanging inequality.

The great chain, its "emanationism and creationism," are eventually replaced by "radical or absolute evolutionism" (317): "The lower precedes the higher, not merely in the history of organic forms and functions, but universally" . . . (317). As he omits all historical and social phenomena, Lovejoy fails to consider so major an event as the French Revolution of 1789 as a factor in the replacement of one dominant idea by another. He attributes change implicitly to the "logical working out of accepted premises" (298), while conceding that he will not attempt to discuss the question of causes for the kind of change he describes. He uses the metaphor of "pressure":

> The pressure of the principle of plenitude can be shown to be a major factor in the great change in presuppositions which becomes most clearly manifest in the religious ideas and the moral and aesthetic ideals and enthusiasms of the generation of German writers who came to maturity between the seventies and the nineties and which were (chiefly) by them communicated to the rest of the world.
>
> [p. 298]

Lovejoy finds in Schelling the introduction of "a radical evolutionism into metaphysics and theology . . ."; the "originally complete and immutable Chain of Being" . . . is "converted into a Becoming . . ." (325-6). Lovejoy calls this "the logically inevitable outcome" (326). The hypothesis of a chain of being was a "failure" because "the hypothesis of the absolute rationality of the cosmos" is "unbelievable" (329). Lovejoy may seem a distant figure; his seminal book on the great chain was presented as a series of lectures in 1932-33. Yet he is the founding father of the history of ideas, and his work is still widely read in universities as an exemplary text in intellectual history. Lovejoy's work reveals, with great clarity, the profound influence of the idea of hierarchy in Western culture.

Other works on the problem, for example the work of David Brion Davis, *The Problem of Slavery in Western Culture*, share some of the same problems I attribute to Lovejoy.[30] Like other historians of Western culture, these authors treat the problem of hierarchy as one which begins at the earliest with Plato. Davis focuses primarily on Aristotle as the first thinker seriously to consider the question of slavery.[31] Modern writers on these questions tend to ignore not only the contributions of the pre-Socratics but also the social situation and background of these thinkers.[32] They treat Plato and Aristotle as the absolute origin of thinking on various topics, when in fact the fourth-century philosophers come at the end of a long debate, after the experiment of democracy had been rejected by conservative thinkers like the philosophers.

I want therefore to provide background to the thinking of these philosophers, to show that they wrote in a historical and philosophical situation. There is a prehistory to the great chain of being. This point seems a necessary corrective even to Davis. More importantly, I want to show how the formulations of Plato and Aristotle mark a break, a discontinuity with the fifth-century speculation about difference, and to describe the nature of that rupture.

The question of prehistory involves a shift from one discursive formation to another, from polarity and analogy to logic and hierarchy. It may be possible to account for this shift simply in terms of autonomous change, of the working out of tools for thinking about thinking. As interesting as the description of the stage previous to Plato and Aristotle—for who can claim to arrive at the true origin of these questions, since there is always a prior stage?—is the reconstruction and description of thinking about difference during an important era in human history, the experiment in democracy of the fifth century B.C.

The necessity for taking up this history at this moment is related to the supremacy of Platonic and Aristotelian formulations in the progress of Western philosophy after them.[33] Let me cite the last words of Lovejoy in *The Great Chain of Being.*

> I may, therefore, perhaps best bring these lectures to a close by a reminder that the idea of the Chain of Being, with its pre-suppositions and implications, has had many curiously happy consequences in the history of Western thought.
>
> [p. 333]

The kind of thinking he describes is not dead; it occurs not simply in the autonomous realms of theology and philosophy.[34] It has direct consequences, in the sense that it rationalizes and justifies an order in the world in which some beings in the hierarchy dominate others, with a comfortable sense of their innate superiority, given them "by nature" or by God.[35] I will repeat here just one example of such thinking, the reflections of the eighteenth century thinker Jenyns cited by Lovejoy:

Animal life rises from this low beginning in the shellfish, through innumerable species of insects, fishes, birds, and beasts, to the confines of reason, where in the dog, the monkey, and chimpanzè, it unites so closely with the lowest degree of that quality in man, that they cannot easily be distinguished from each other. From this lowest degree in the brutal Hottentot, reason, with the assistance of learning and science, advances, through the various stages of human understanding. . . .[36]

The brutal Hottentot was a favorite of the period. Lovejoy mentions Sir John Ovington, who calls the Hottentots "the very Reverse of Human kind . . . so that if there's any medium between a Rational Animal and a Beast, the Hottentot lays the fairest claim to that species."[37] Sir William Petty says the "Negros who live about the Cape of Good Hope are the most beastlike of all the Sorts of Men with whom our travellers are well acquainted."[38]

Men who are like beasts can be treated as beasts. Jenyns' remarks on reason come very close to those of Plato on *logos*, and it must be remembered that not only *barbaroi*, foreigners, were seen by Plato to be deprived of reasoning ability. Women and slaves as well as animals formed part of a "chain" which descended from the Ideas, from the Idea of the good, from god. The hierarchy which Plato fixed among kinds endured for many centuries and still operates in Western discourse about difference.

My purpose then, is to describe the context in which Plato and Aristotle invent the chain, to show the rupture their thinking makes with the fifth-century past, in a way which illuminates the historical specificity of the great chain. The clarification of ideas of superiority and inferiority in terms of sexual, racial, and species difference is an important step in the history of Western philosophy and of social relations in the Western world. It justifies relations of dominance and submission for those who follow in the tradition.

To make sense of the system of speculation in the fifth century, it will be necessary to consider not only philosophical but literary and artistic "texts" as well. The public art of the democratic *polis* is the realm in which the ideas of difference were played out, the space in which men learned to define themselves as male, Greek, human, as citizens in a community from which the other—female, barbarian, animal—was excluded.

Lovejoy's founding work, *The Great Chain*, describes the history of the idea of hierarchy in Western discourse. I would like to follow him in this project, but to supplement his approach with the critique of Michel Foucault in his "archaeology of knowledge." Foucault in fact has studied what Lovejoy called the "dialectical motive" of an age, in his work *Les mots et les choses*. There he reconstructs in an "archaeology" three periods in recent Western history.[39] In the *Archéologie du savoir*, Foucault situates his own theoretical project very explicitly in opposition to that of the historians of ideas and lists four crucial points of divergence from them: "the attribution of innovation, the analysis of contradictions, comparative descriptions, and the mapping of transformations."[40] He proposes, in place of the history of ideas, the analysis of the *episteme*:

> By *episteme*, we mean, in fact, the total set of relations that unite, at a given period, the discursive practices that give rise to epistemological figures, sciences, and possibly formalized systems: the way in which, in each of the discursive formations, the transitions to epistemologization, scientificity, and formalization are situated and operate; the distribution of these thresholds, which may coincide, be subordinated to one another, or be separated by shifts in time; the lateral relations that may exist between epistemological figures of sciences in so far as they belong to neighbouring, but distinct, discursive practices.[41]

The many dimensions of such an analysis are beyond the scope of this study. Foucault himself has not succeeded in presenting us with an exemplary "archaeology." And I am interested not simply in the *episteme* of the fifth and fourth centuries B.C. nor in polarity and analogy, but rather in the specific problem of the prehistory and invention of the great chain of being as speculation about difference among kinds.

Yet Foucault's prescription for cultural history contains important correctives to the sort of analysis done traditionally by historians of ideas. In particular, his emphasis on the *total set of relations uniting discursive practices* points up some of the problems in the history of ideas as practiced by Lovejoy. At times in *The Great Chain*, in part because of the immensity of the task he has undertaken, Lovejoy fails to take into account the specificity of whole systems of thought in which particular conceptions are embedded, and in which they "mean."[42]

Foucault's concept of change is both instructive, and ultimately limited. He is critical of a "concern for continuities, transitions, anticipations, and fore-shadowings." "Rather than refer to the living force of change (as if it were its own principle), rather than seek its causes (as if it were no more than a mere effect) archaeology tries to establish the system of transformations that constitute 'change. . . .' "[43] The difficulty is that while the history of ideas seems to use a model of continuous evolution, a constant line of development towards the present, the "archaeological" model affirms an arbitrary broken course for the history of thought, one in which there can be no explanation for change. This is not an entirely satisfactory model.[44] It is nonetheless a model the emphasis of which serves my purposes well, in part because it brings into high relief a particular feature of the transformation between the world of the fifth-century *polis* and the period of the fourth century. It may seem an exaggeration to speak of a rupture, a break, a discontinuity between these two worlds, yet clearly a significant transformation did occur, if only on the level of genre, as I pointed out above. The "epistemological" model then is useful, not as a falsification of the realities of this history, but as one which brings to the foreground certain aspects of the history of thought which are crucial to my enterprise.

Foucault's "archaeology" is not the history of the Zeitgeist. He himself points out that he is not concerned with what he calls "total history."[45] The very fact of the complexity of "archaeological" study—its concern with "series, divisions, limits, differences of level, shifts, chronological specificities"—makes that wholeness a myth which has been superseded. I would not pretend here to be writing a total history, nor even what is called a *general* history, one that relates all these series to one another. I am concerned with a single problem, the idea of difference, and how it is articulated at various discursive levels in the classical age. Thus my method attempts to integrate those of Lovejoy and Foucault. It draws on modern anthropological theory as well, especially the work of Claude Lévi-Strauss, his followers and critics. The research of structural anthropologists on kinship and on mythology can be of great interest to classical scholars; a groundbreaking work like Detienne's *Les jardins d'Adonis* depends on the theoretical advances of Lévi-Strauss.[46]

I will argue in this "history," that the transformation from analogical to hierarchical thinking can be related to social conflict, to the collapse of a particular form of political organization in the wake of the devastation of the Peloponnesian War.[47] There is a radical discontinuity in thinking about difference which marks a change from fifth-century to fourth-century discourse, and that shift is related to political and social change. The change in genres, in logic, in audience, is a symptom of this discontinuity.

If the history of a culture is in question, one cannot rely simply on literary documents. My concern here is to show how artistic monuments as well as literary, historical and philosophical texts were part of the same universe of discourse. Part of Lovejoy's enterprise was to break down the artificial barriers between kinds of study,[48] yet his heirs have come to the practice of the history of ideas failing even to consider the literary qualities of a work of verbal art. They have at times simply extracted the relevant "unit-idea" and gone on to plunder another text. Clearly, if one is to respect the synchrony of a particular "discursive formation," if one is to understand the place of an "idea" in its context, one must consider the works of art and thought of a period in their complex inter-relationship. This is difficult in practice, but it must remain an ideal. I will discuss works of plastic art as well as verbal art, especially public works like the Athenian treasury at Delphi and the Parthenon, which as much as any other artifacts illustrate the concerns of the classical *polis*. I will consider not only the tragedies of Aeschylus, Sophocles, and Euripides, but will refer also to Aristophanes, to Herodotus and Thucydides, to the pre-Socratics and to Plato and Aristotle.

It might be argued that my choice of literary examples—the *Persae*, the *Trachiniae*, the *Medea*—is limited. These are meant to be examples illustrative of the modes of thinking with which I am concerned. I am not arguing necessarily that they represent a balanced sample of tragic material. The *Persae* is an aberrant play even within the Aeschylean corpus; yet it exemplifies clearly the necessity for separation between Greeks and barbarians. The *Trachiniae* is of interest in part because it reverses the incest themes of *Oedipus Rex*, a play on which so much critical attention has focused since antiquity. The *Medea* is a play of such violence and contradiction that it very well illustrates, by exception, the situation of women in Greek tragedy.

Moreover, there is clearly a chronological development in the choice made. The *Persae* is the earliest and most extreme example of polarizing logic; it was produced in 472, shortly after the Greek victory over the Persians. Pericles was *choregos* for the production; the great period of the democracy, the empire, the construction of the Parthenon, the tragic festivals, intervene between the production of this play and the two which follow in my discussion, the *Trachiniae* and the *Medea*.

The Peloponnesian War, a war between brother Hellenes, ended the peace and stability of the Periclean period. The two tragedies of Sophocles and Euripides were perhaps both produced near the beginning of the war. The date of the *Trachiniae* has been much contested. The argument for a date in the 440's is persuasive to me; but more important than an absolute dating is the contrast between the playwrights. They represent distinct stages in the evolution of Greek speculation about difference. John Finley in his *Four Stages of Greek Thought*, places Sophocles with Aeschylus as exemplary of the "visionary mind," while he groups Euripides and Thucydides in a later stage, the "theoretical mind."[49] The two later tragedians, who were contemporaries and whose works so often reflect an almost dialectical relationship, are nevertheless radically distinct thinkers. Sophocles belongs to the great classical moment, when the *polis* is defining itself and the role of man within it; Euripides, writing at the same moment, sees already the collapse of social harmony and the consequent erosion of definition of like and unlike. Thus even within the period which reasons through analogy and polarity, there is change, which I have tried to illustrate clearly by selecting extreme examples of each stage in the process.

This study is neither a history of Greek tragedy nor a cultural history of the fifth century B.C. It is rather intended to describe discourse concerning difference, and the rupture between the literary and artistic texts of the *polis* and the hierarchizing argumentation of the fourth-century philosophers.[50] Such a study of an *episteme* emphasizes the significance of silences, of discontinuities and repetitions within the discursive formation. The clearest of assumptions in an age are those which are unspoken, which buttress every argument, which form the background of every utterance. In a sense, the study of the transformation of discourse about difference is a case of a silence becoming speech, of a society finding a language in which to speak of things unsaid in the past. Male citizens in the fifth century knew themselves to be different from females, barbarians, animals; the philosophers of the fourth century told them why they were different.

NOTES

1.   On the importance of logos for the entire Western philosophical tradition, see Jean-Marie Benoist, *La tyrannie du logos* (Paris, 1975).

2.   Eric Havelock's work on literacy in the *polis* has wide-reaching significance which has not yet been sufficiently acknowledged by classical scholars. See his *Preface to Plato*, (Oxford, 1963); *The Origins of Western Literacy* (Toronto, 1976); "The Preliteracy of the Greeks," *NLH* 8:3 (Spring, 1977): 369-91: "High classical Greek literature is to be viewed as composed in a condition of increasing tension between the modes of oral and documented speech" [371]; and *The Greek Concept of Justice* (Cambridge, Mass. and London, 1978).

3.   See F.M. Cornford, *From Religion to Philosophy* (London, 1912); Havelock, *Preface*; F. Solmsen, *Intellectual Experiments of the Greek Enlightenment* (Princeton, 1975); E.R. Dodds, *The Greeks and The Irrational* (Berkeley and Los Angeles, 1951).

4.   Jean-Pierre Vernant and Pierre Vidal-Naquet, *Mythe et tragédie en Grèce ancienne* (Paris, 1972):

> L'univers tragique se situe entre deux mondes, et c'est cette double référence au mythe . . . et aux valeurs nouvelles développées avec tant de rapidité par la cité de Peisistrate, de

Clisthène, de Thémistocle, de Périclès, qui constitue une de ses originalités, et le ressort même de l'action.

[8]

See also *Les origines de la pensée grecque*, 2nd rev. ed., (Paris, 1969); and *Mythe et pensée chez les grecs, études de psychologie historique*, 2nd ed. (Paris, 1966).

5. *Mythe et tragédie*, pp. 34-36.

6. A ce dédoublement du choeur et du héros tragiques correspond, dans la langue même de la tragédie, une dualité: d'une part, le lyrisme choral; d'autre part, chez les protagonistes du drame, une forme dialoguée dont la métrique est plus voisine à la prose.

[14]

See also "Greek Tragedy: Problems of Interpretation" in *The Languages of Criticism and the Sciences of Man*, ed. by R. Macksey and E. Donato (Baltimore, 1971), pp. 273-89: "Tragedy . . . in its formal logic on the most abstract level, is a passage between mythic thought and philosophic thought, between Hesiod and Aristotle" [289]. On Sophocles, see also, "Ambiguity and Reversal: On the Enigmatic Structure of *Oedipus Rex*," trans. by P. duBois, *NLH* 9:3 (Spring 1978): 475-501.

7. On the history of this transition, and for useful bibliographical material, see Perry Anderson, *Passages from Antiquity to Feudalism* (London, 1974).

8. For a description of the career of Alexander, see W.W. Tarn, *Alexander the Great* (Cambridge, 1948).

9. G.E.R. Lloyd, *Polarity and Analogy, Two Types of Argumentation in Early Greek Thought* (Cambridge, 1966), p. 434. Polarity is the relating or reducing phenomena to a pair or pair of opposite principles; analogy is assimilating or likening one (unknown) object to another that seems better known [436].

Although Lloyd has received criticism for over-emphasizing polarity and analogy, for reducing the complex dialectic of Greek thought to two simple mechanisms, he usefully points to a dominant mode of reasoning for the period he discusses.

10. Ibid., p. 193. Using the metaphor of the cosmos as a state, Heraclitus saw it as anarchy, Parmenides and Empedocles as an oligarchy or a limited democracy, and Plato as a monarchy [213].

11. Chapter 5, "The Pre-Philosophical Background," traces the polarizing and analogical theories of cosmologists and biologists, while Lloyd's conclusion, "The Development of Logic and Methodology in Early Greek Thought," discusses the innovations

of Aristotle—refinements in argument such as logical necessity, logical impossibility, probability, and the use of evidence.

12.   Arthur O. Lovejoy, *The Great Chain of Being, A Study of the History of an Idea* (Cambridge, Mass., 1936), 13th printing, 1976, p. 10. For the history of ideas of ancient culture, see Jeremy L. Tobey, *The History of Ideas: A Bibliographical Introduction*, vol. 1, *Classical Antiquity* (Santa Barbara and Oxford, 1975). The most significant model for a synthetic and historically penetrating study of "ideas" is Roy Harvey Pearce's *Savagism and Civilization, A Study of the Indian and the American Mind*, first published as *The Savages of America: A Study of the Indian and the Idea of Civilization* (Baltimore, 1953), revised ed. (Baltimore, 1965). Pearce traces in an exemplary fashion the dialectic between historical events and human consciousness in American culture.

13.   Jacques Derrida, "Différance," in *Speech and Phenomenon and Other Essays on Husserl's Theory of Signs*, trans. by D.B. Allison, pref. by N. Garner, (Evanston, 1973), p. 129. The essay was first published in the *Bulletin de la société française de la philosophie* 62 (1968). As Derrida points out, the Greek *diapherô* is more restricted in meaning than Latin *differre*, which includes the notion of postponement [136]. The vision of a system of differences is crucial to the Saussurean theory of language:

> In language there are only differences without positive terms. Whether we take the signified or the signifier, language has neither ideas nor sounds that existed before the linguistic system, but only conceptual and phonic differences that have issued from the system.

F. de Saussure, *Course in General Linguistics*, ed. by C. Bally, A. Sechehaye, and A. Riedlinger, trans. by W. Baskin (New York, 1966), p. 120. I would argue that in the system of differentiations I am discussing, which refers to kinds of beings, the system changes as "reality" changes.

14.   Diogenes Laertius, *Lives of Eminent Philosophers*, with English translation by R.D. Hicks, 2 vols., (London [Loeb], 1925). Although the anecdote is told of both Thales and Socrates, and reported by this late source, the analogical model it lays out is consistent with other evidence in fifth-century culture.

15.   John H. Finley, Jr., *Pindar and Aeschylus* (Cambridge, Mass., 1955).

16.   *Geschichte des Altertums*, 3rd ed. (Stuttgart, 1939), IV, pp. 423-33.

17.   On the myth of the invention of women, see Pietro Pucci, *Hesiod and the Language of Poetry* (Baltimore and London, 1977),

pp. 82 ff.; Nicole Loraux, "Sur la race des femmes et quelques-unes de ses tribus," *Arethusa* 11:1, 2 (1978): 43-87; J.-P. Vernant, "Le mythe hésiodique des races," *Mythe et pensée*, pp. 13-79, and "Le mythe prométhéen chez Hésiode," in *Mythe et société en Grèce ancienne* (Paris, 1974) pp. 177-94.

18.   Hans Schwabl *et alii*, *Grecs et barbares* (Entretiens Hardt, vol. 8) (Geneva, 1962). See also E.E. Sikes, *The Anthropology of the Greeks* (London, 1914).

19.   Baldry's work is an excellent summary of Greek attitudes toward the barbarians, from Homer to Alexander and beyond. H.C. Baldry, *The Unity of Mankind in Greek Thought* (Cambridge, 1965).

20.   Havelock's work has been insufficiently appreciated.   He argues that:

> . . . early Ionian science included as a central element in its speculations a fairly coherent theory of the origins of human society, technology, and civilization, itself based on a theory of the development of man as a species out of previous species, a theory which can fairly be described as naturalist and evolutionary, in sharp contrast to the typological reasoning of Plato and Aristotle. . . . Long before the Hellenistic age, Greek political theory was prepared to indicate the ground rules for a society in which the city-state was incidental, not essential, in which law was built up by human convention and rendered viable by the historical process, rather than derived from divine archetypes; a society in which language functioned as a vehicle of communication and of persuasion, by which men working on each other continually formulated common goals and purposes. The very different theories of Plato and Aristotle, so far from being a summation of previous Greek thinking in this department, were designed to counteract its effects, or more properly to call up the forces of an older order of Greek ideas to correct the balance of the new.

Eric Havelock, *The Liberal Temper in Greek Politics* (New Haven and London, 1957), pp. 5-6. Havelock's assessment of the role of Plato and Aristotle is close to my own; we differ in that I am concerned with the widespread speculation about difference among kinds manifest in verbal and graphic art, while he treats what he calls "Greek anthropology" [31].

21.   Cole demonstrates the likelihood of a lost late fifth-century theory of cultural origins, probably derived from a source in

Democritus, by considering subsequent texts. Thomas Cole, *Democritus and the Sources of Greek Anthropology* (Princeton, 1967).

22. Bruno Snell, *The Discovery of the Mind. The Greek Origins of European Thought*, trans. by T.G. Rosenmeyer (New York, 1960). See also A. Gouldner, *Enter Plato, Classical Greece and the Origins of Social Theory* (New York, 1965).

23. John H. Finley, Jr., *Four Stages of Greek Thought* (Stanford, 1966).

24. J.-P. Vernant, *Les origines. . . .*, and Marcel Detienne, *Les maîtres de vérité dans la Grèce archaïque*, 2nd ed. (Paris, 1973).

25. J.-P. Vernant and Marcel Detienne, *Les ruses de l'intelligence: la mètis des grecs* (Paris, 1974).

26. Marcel Detienne, *Les jardins d'Adonis* (Paris, 1972).

27. René Girard, *La violence et le sacré* (Paris, 1972). Girard seems to argue for the inevitability of both violence and hierarchy, in all cultures.

28. Robert Schlaifer, "Greek Theories of Slavery from Homer to Aristotle," *HSCP* 47 (1936): 165-204; G.R. Morrow, *Plato's Law of Slavery*, University of Illinois Studies in Language and Literature 25, 3 (1939); M.I. Finley, "Was Greek Civilization Based on Slave Labour?" *Historia* 8 (1959): 145-64, and *The Ancient Economy* (Berkeley and Los Angeles, 1973). See also the collection of essays edited by Finley, which contains further bibliographical material: *Slavery in Classical Antiquity: Views and Controversies* (Cambridge, 1960).

29. Joseph Vogt, *Ancient Slavery and the Ideal of Man*, trans. by T. Weidemann (Oxford, 1974). See especially the bibliographical supplement, pp. 211-17. Earlier, see *Bibliographie zur antiken Sklaverei*, ed. J. Vogt and N. Brockmeyer (Bochum, 1971), and the series *Forschungen zur antiken Sklaverei* (Mainz, from 1967); H. Kuch, *Kriegsgefangenschaft und Sklaverei bei Euripides* (dissertation, Humboldt University, Berlin, 1970); P. Vidal-Naquet, "Esclavage et gynécocratie," in *Recherches sur les structures sociales dans l'antiquité classique* (CNRS) (Paris, 1970), 63-80; and J.-P. Vernant, "La lutte des classes," in *Mythe et société . . .*, pp. 17 ff.; E. Lepore, "Economia antica e storiografia moderna," in *Ricerche storiche ed economiche in memoria di Corrado Barbagallo* I (Naples, 1970), pp. 1 ff.

30. Davis' excellent survey focuses on slavery in America, but traces the Hebraic and classical civilizations' attitudes to the problem in chapter 3, "Slavery and Sin: The Ancient Legacy," *The Problem of Slavery in Western Culture* (Ithaca, 1966).

31. Ibid., pp. 69-72.

32. See, for example: Ashley Montagu, *Man's Most Dangerous Myth: The Fallacy of Race*, 4th ed. (Cleveland and New York, 1964).

33. See, for example, Michele le Doeff, "Women and Philosophy," in *Radical Philosophy* 17 (Summer 1977), *Arethusa* 6:1 (Spring 1973), on "Women and Antiquity," and the call for study of Plato and Aristotle, by John Peradotto, the editor of a special edition of *Arethusa* devoted to "Women in the Ancient World,": "It is regrettable that we have here no study of Plato and Aristotle, in whom the Greek cognitive system is most open to awareness of alternatives and most fully available to analysis." *Arethusa* 11:1, 2, (1978) p. 5.

34. Ideas about the innate inferiority of females and racial minorities are obviously still wide-spread in the culture as a whole, and in all academic fields, not only in sociobiology and genetics.

35. Roy Harvey Pearce, op. cit., on the victory of civilization over Savagism in America. See also E. Benveniste, "Civilisation: Contribution à l'histoire du mot," in *Problèmes de linguistique générale*, vol. 1 (Paris, 1966), pp. 336 ff.

36. Cited in Lovejoy, op. cit., p. 197.

37. Ibid., p. 234.

38. Ibid., n. 17, p. 363.

39. Michel Foucault, *Les mots et les choses, une archéologie des sciences humaines* (Paris, 1966). Translated as *The Order of Things* (London, 1967).

40. Michel Foucault, *L'Archéologie du savoir* (Paris, 1969). Translated as *The Archeology of Knowledge* (London, 1972), p. 138.

41. Ibid., p. 191.

42. His discussion of Plato, for example, is restricted essentially to the Theory of the Ideas, with more stress given to its consequences in Western thought than to the whole body of Platonic theory. This is not a criticism *per se*, since his object of analysis is the tradition of this concept; however, the focus on synchrony brings other features to prominence.

43. Foucault, *Archaeology*, p. 173. "Archaeology is much more willing than the history of ideas to speak of discontinuities, ruptures, gaps, entirely new forms of positivity, and of sudden redistributions" [169].

44. On this question, see Fredric Jameson, *The Prison-house of Language* (Princeton, 1972).

45. Foucault, *Archaeology*, p. 9.

46. On Durkheim, Gernet, Vernant, and the application of modern anthropological theory to classical civilization, see S.C. Humphreys, *Anthropology and the Greeks* (London, 1978).

47. Thus I violate Foucault's prescriptions in several ways: I do not accept discourse simply as a fact of language, but "question things said as to what they are hiding, what they were 'really' saying, in spite of themselves, the unspoken element that they contain. . . ." [109]. This process seems a necessary and inevitable one, especially in dealing with imaginative rather than "scientific" texts. Unlike Foucault, whose concern is with entire "discursive formations," I treat a single phenomenon which manifests itself in many "discursive formations." Furthermore, I seek to find causes for the rupture in thinking about difference in fifth- and fourth-century discourse.

48. Lovejoy, op. cit., pp. 16-17.

49. Finley, *Four Stages*, pp. 28-79.

50. For a class analysis of the works of Plato and Aristotle, see E.M. Wood and N. Wood, *Class Ideology and Ancient Political Theory* (Oxford, 1978).

I

Centaurs and Amazons

Since the transformation at issue here involves a shift from implicit to explicit reasoning about difference, it is necessary to describe the earlier period's assumptions without reference to explicit statements on the subject.[1] The statement of Thales about his good fortune is one mode of self-definition. This first chapter will discuss other modes of speculation about differentiation and self-definition, in order to generate categories with which to examine several literary works of the fifth century. The focus will be primarily on the public art of the city of Athens, that is, monumental art, and on tragedy, because they were the most communal of texts. They represent utterances on questions which concerned the body politic, and are thus ideal for discovering speculation about those outside that body.

Although there exist pre-Socratic philosophical fragments, for the most part they lack the coherence and accessibility of the literary documents, many of them represent points of view from outside the democratic city of Athens, and there are difficulties in attributing an audience, a social context, to these texts. A thinker like Heraclitus, one of the most remarkable of Western philosophers, concerned himself obliquely with questions that are taken up systematically in the fourth century. Yet he did so in an extraordinarily veiled and oracular manner, and the thrust of his thinking involves a consideration of cosmological and cosmogonic issues which, although they are often metaphorically related to political or social speculation, are beyond the scope of this study.[2]

The great lyric poet Pindar too, although a contemporary of Aeschylus, is concerned less than the tragedians with the mythical hero's relationship to a community and more with the heroic patron's approach to the divine. For example, in the First Olympian, a magnificent *epinikion* written for Hieron, tyrant of

25

Syracuse, Pindar begins with a priamel cataloguing substances of extraordinary purity and brilliance:

> Even as water is most excellent [*ariston men hudôr*] while gold, like fire gleaming at night, gleams more brightly than all other lordly wealth . . .[3]
>
> [1-2]

The poet goes on to link analogically the Olympian games, Hieron, Pelops. One of the themes of the poem is that the divine is outside the human world, yet the rare experience of connection with it is what gives meaning to the *personae* of Pindar's poetic universe.[4] Pindar is an encomiast; his poetry is concerned with establishing bonds, often through analogy, between the gods and the best of men. Pelops was loved by Poseidon; Tantalus, his father, proved unworthy of the gods' favor; Pelops returned to live among men and won a first athletic victory in his race for Hippodameia. Hieron is praised for his likeness to these mythical heroes, and the poet ends his song with a hope for future victories for the Sicilian king:

> . . . the crowning summit is for kings [*to d'eschaton koruphoutai basileusi*]. Refrain from peering too far! Heaven grant that you may plant your feet on high, so long as you live, and that I may consort with victors for all my days, and be foremost in the lore of song among Hellenes in every land.
>
> [113-116]

Pindar uses analogy brilliantly to associate himself with the king, with the heroes, with the purest of elements he listed in the poem's first lines. He is concerned with the best, the *aristoi*, those excellent things and men standing above the insignificant mass.

For Pindar, the universe is divided between god and man; his thinking and his images, analogically structured as they clearly are, belong to a world which precedes that of the democracy. Tragedy, with its complex examination of the hero and his community, of their interdependence, is born in the city. There we find the model of analogy as it is used to define the human community, the *polis* as a unit. Such analogical discourse begins with tragedy, the city's moving reinterpretation of its mythic tradition.

Myths are tales of gods, heroes, of a time before the one in which men find themselves. At the heart of the Pindaric discourse are myths such as those told of Pelops and Tantalus; elsewhere, in *Pythian* 2, he tells the tale of the Centaurs. Pindar elaborates myth within the context of his encomia, to link men with the gods. The *polis* inherits the same body of mythic material, including the Centaur tale, and works it into a very different discourse. The tragedians of the fifth century receive tales from the archaic, aristocratic world, and use them to speculate about the nature of their own community.

Beginning then, with myth, the most public of genres, since there is no fixed version of a myth[5]—it is available to be interpreted and reworked by every teller—I will discuss some principles which emerge from a study of the stories told by Pindar and others, of Centaurs and Amazons, and then examine their representation in works of art of the fifth century, especially the civic monuments of Athens. From this analysis of myth and its representation, categories appear through which it is possible to analyze similar patterns in the tragic literary art of the fifth century.

In the myths of the Greeks, the Amazons and the Centaurs were creatures at the boundaries of difference. Speculation about them constitutes part of the Greeks' thinking about sexual, cultural, and species boundaries. The Centaurs were beings on the threshold between human and equine nature; they marked the limit between animal and human being, between *anthrôpos* and *thêrion*. The Centaur appears first on Kassite boundary stones as a guardian of limits; he developed in Near Eastern thought into the astrological figure Sagittarius. In Greek myth the Centaurs descended from Ixion, as did their traditional opponents, the Lapiths. Ixion married Dia, daughter of Eioneus, but instead of giving his father-in-law the bride-price, Ixion set for him a trap of burning coals.[6]

Marcel Detienne points out in *Les jardins d'Adonis* that the Centaurs operate within a mythological code defining reproduction and marriage in opposition to promiscuous sexuality.[7] Pindar recounts how the Centaurs from their very origins were associated with the negation of marriage. Ixion, unable to find a mortal to absolve him of his crime, was finally accepted as a suppliant by Zeus. But Ixion, true to his anti-marriage character, attempted to seduce Zeus' sister and wife Hera.[8] He instead had intercourse with Nephele—cloud—an *eidôlon* of Hera, and begat either the first Centaur, or Centauros, who subsequently, after intercourse with a mare, became the father of the Centaurs.[9] Ixion, in punishment for his act, was bound to a wheel which burned and turned eternally first in the air, then in the underworld.[10] Detienne compares his turning to that of the *iunx*, the instrument of magical seduction.[11]

In many of the episodes in the Centaur myth, the horse/men sustained Ixion's hostility to legal marriage and to the forms of exchange typical of Greek civilization. In the earliest tellings of the myth, those concerning Herakles, Centaurs consistently violated relations of *xenia*, guest-friendship. In his pursuit of the Erymanthian Boar, one of the canonical *athloi*, Herakles encountered the Centaur Pholos, who received and fed the hero.[12] The host was reluctant to serve the stranger wine from the common store of the Centaurs, but was persuaded. The rest of the Centaurs, smelling the wine, appeared and began a battle with Herakles. They destroyed the relationship of *xenia* established between Pholos and the hero.

The scene marked the centaurs as both greedy and incapable of receiving guests, as uncivilized as Polyphemos in the *Odyssey*. In addition, as G.S. Kirk has shown, they were bestial and drunken, incapable of controlling themselves after smelling the fermented liquids.[13] They gave violence, not gifts to their guest, and the fermented grape, a substance neither raw nor cooked, was too much for their wild, raw nature—they reverted to the animal side of their being. Pholos, in contact with culture through Herakles, could tolerate the substance, but he was swept away in their animal riot. The deaths of both Cheiron and Pholos, the most human of Centaurs, can be traced to this episode. Pholos wounded himself fatally with one of Herakles' poisoned arrows, Cheiron too received such a wound, and it proved so painful that he traded his immortality to Prometheus in order to die and be released. Thus this episode of the myth forced the Centaurs further from association with humans. They were represented as uncivilized and incapable of relations with human beings. Anticulture personified, they could not tolerate among them even the most bestial of heroes, Herakles.

Another important episode of the Centaur myth, the Centaur Nessos' attempt to abduct Herakles' bride Deianeira, will be considered in depth later in an analysis of Sophocles' *Trachiniae*. Other episodes concerned not Herakles but the Athenian hero Theseus, who frequently replaced Herakles in myth. Theseus' comrade in arms, Peirithoös, son of Dia and Zeus, invited the Centaurs to join him in the celebration of his marriage to Hippodameia. After drinking wine and coming into contact with human women, the Centaurs ran wild and tried to carry off the Lapith women, Hippodameia among them. The battle which ensued, the Centauromachy, resulted in the defeat of the Centaurs, but not before Kaineus, a male hero who had gone through a sex change after having been raped as a female by Poseidon, was destroyed, though immortal, by being pressed into the earth by the Centaurs.[14] In this version of the myth, as in the tale of Herakles with Pholos, the Centaurs violated ordered festivity. They consistently refused to respect the relationships of orderly exchange—that is, gift-exchange and the exchange of women, marriage—which were seen by the Greeks as well as by Claude Lévi-Strauss to found human culture and to differentiate humans from beasts.

Cheiron, the most important exception to the bestial conduct of the tribe of Centaurs, was tutor to many of the Greek heroes, including both Herakles and Achilles.[15] Alone among the horse/men, his ancestry was traced back to the union of Kronos with the Oceanid Philyra. His form—half horse, half man—was attributed either to Kronos' appearing to Philyra disguised as a horse, or to Philyra's attempt to escape by turning herself into a mare. Cheiron's mother, horrified by the shape of her offspring, was changed into a lime tree by Zeus.[16] Cheiron was the only Centaur to be immortal, to be married; he shared his vast knowledge of hunting with the heroes entrusted to his care. He also possessed knowledge about *pharmaka*, drugs, and taught his craft to his pupils. Cheiron's benevolence shows how the Centaurs inhabited a threshold, were liminal in another sense; that is,

they lived in nature both as violent, uncivilized beasts, and as
characters from a lost past, before the necessity for a separation
between gods and men, before work, cooking, death, all the evils
that culture brings. They demonstrate the Greeks' fundamental
ambivalence about nature and about the prehistory of mankind.
The world before culture was viewed with nostalgia as well as
loathing.

In representations in art, as P. Baur has shown in his important work, *Centaurs in Ancient Art* (still useful although first published in 1912), Cheiron expressed his double identity.[17] He was
shown as having a normal human body, draped like a Greek's,
with the addition of a horse's back, hind legs, and tail. The other
Centaurs are most frequently shown naked, with varying degrees
of shagginess. In some representations, as on the cylix described
by Baur (242, belonging to his category B, Centaurs with human
forelegs), the Centaurs have human genitals, while other Centaurs
have only horse genitals:

> Sometimes only the human part is shaggy . . . (sometimes)
> only the equine part is shaggy. A technical peculiarity of all
> Centaurs in the geometric period . . . (is that) the human
> forelegs are added to the equine body without indicating the
> buttocks. In later times an equine body is attached to a com-
> pletely human figure. On the geometric monuments, how-
> ever, human forelegs take the place of equine forelegs, the
> human torso not connected with them, but growing out of
> the equine body. Therefore the human pudenda are lack-
> ing.[18]

Baur lists also, as number 238, a bronze statue from the Acropolis
now in the National Museum in Athens, which had both "equine
pudenda" and "human pudenda," now missing.[19]

Georges Dumézil sees the Centaurs as having a temporal
liminality—he associates them with the Sanskrit Gandarvah:

> . . . ces génies étaient bien des génies de changement
> d'année ou de fin d'hiver et . . . à travers les différences
> commandées par les siècles et les lieux, ils avaient toujours
> les multiples caractères ordinaires à génies de cette catégorie:

génies de la nature, génies du monde des morts, génies du temps . . .[20]

As liminal characters, the Centaurs may be understood most fully if their sexual nature is taken into account. They are not simply nature spirits, or river creatures, but also hybrid monsters whose existence in myth permitted speculation about boundaries and kinds. The Centaurs formed an asymmetrical, overly masculine, violently bestial alternative to the norm of what was seen by the Greeks as human culture. They were hyper-masculine; the violence and sexuality of horses was super-added to human virility in their bodies.

The work done recently by Jeffrey Henderson on obscene language in Aristophanes adds support to the view of the Centaurs as sexually charged beings. He notes that "*kentron*, any point or goad, was common for phallus,"[21] *tauros* frequently meant phallus,[22] and "cunt" as well,[23] *kentein* alluded to a position in intercourse in which "the woman bends backwards and thrusts her hips forward. As a sexual term this word always includes rapid pelvic motion, whether as part of a seductive dance or actually in coitus."[24] The ambiguity of the term is interesting, although in either case, whether referring to intercourse between male and female or between male and male, it suits the sexual aggressivity of the Centaur and is appropriate to the folk etymology for the name Centaur. In the compound, the term *Kentauros* refers to "aggressive (as opposed to pathic) homosexuals . . . ," as at *Clouds* 346 and 350.[25]

Female Centaurs in art, in the period discussed by Baur and later, were relatively rare.[26] The Centaurs were male in the extreme, and even their attributes of drunkenness and lust corresponded to certain Greek notions of undiluted masculinity. If Herakles was the exemplar of archaic virility and *aretê*, the Centaurs represented a more instinctive version of his intense maleness which was brought into high relief by inversion in the representation of Herakles enslaved to Omphale. The Centaurs shared some attributes with the satyrs, who also travelled in groups and were known for unbridled desire and an intolerance for wine. The satyrs too had horses' tails, and were often depicted in art carrying women off in postures very like those of the raping centaurs. In the fifth century, the lustful centaur Eurythion showed the phallic displacement onto the tail which is characteristic of representations of the satyrs.[27] The centaurs had few female companions, few females of their own kind, and this lack, coupled with a half-bestial nature, accounts for their chaotic, rapacious behavior in the incidents involving Herakles, Theseus, and the Lapiths.

The myth of the Centaurs, as well as its frequent representation on vases, seals, amulets, and sculpture, was part of the speculation about difference that characterized Greek thought of the fifth century B.C. As liminal beings, half-horse, half-men, they tested the boundaries between man and beast, between nature and culture. In addition, they raised the question of male and female difference, since their bodies and their behavior indicated that they were an exclusively masculine species, doubly potent in possessing the sexual attributes of both human male and animal. There was no account of reproduction of the Centaur species. They engaged in hunting, drinking, and fighting without any suggestion of domestic life or of reproduction through female Centaurs, until quite late. Thus the myth is an ideal one for reflection on the nature of human and animal, male and female. I will show how this speculation occurs later in this chapter.

First, however, let us consider another myth which shares some of the characteristics of the Centaur myth, in that it touches on boundary creatures and hostility to marriage, and establishes the possibility of another cultural alternative to that of the Greek *polis*. Although the Amazons seem far distant from the Centaurs, they are in many ways bound up in the same implicit process of speculating about difference.

Like the Centaurs, the Amazons were involved in the myths told about both Herakles and Theseus, as well as other heroic figures.[28] Bellerophon, a hero with tasks to fulfill, fought the Amazons as well as the Solymoi and the Chimaera. This latter monster, one third lion, one third dragon, one third goat, was a hybrid being not unlike the Amazons, who shared male and female attributes. Although Bellerophon defeated the female band of Amazons, he in turn was defeated by the Xanthian women, who lifted their skirts and used the apotropaic power of their genitals to drive him away from their city.[29]

The Amazons also entered the stories concerning the great hero Achilles. An alternate ending to the traditional last line of the *Iliad* was one which announced the coming of the Amazons to the aid of the Trojans, although Priam says in Book III that in his youth he fought against them (*Iliad* 3.159). The tradition of their involvement in the war was alluded to in the frieze on the temple of Juno in the *Aeneid* and in the *Post-Homerica* of Quintus Smyrnaeus; it was evidently the subject of one of the cyclic poems, the *Aithiopis* of Arktinos of Miletus.[30] According to tradition, the queen of the Amazons, Penthesilea, was killed in combat by Achilles, who fell in love with her as she died. The hero later killed Thersites because he mocked Achilles' passion for the Amazon.

Herakles acquired the girdle of the Amazons as one of his canonical labors. Versions of this episode differ; in some he took an army with him to the Amazons' territory, variously placed in the eastern and northern regions of the Black Sea. In other versions he went alone, to join combat with Hippolyta or Melanippe, and won the girdle as the prize for his victory.[31] Sometimes Theseus was said to have accompanied him on his journey and to have abducted Antiope, also known as Hippolyta.[32] The girdle which Herakles acquired was shown in classical times in the temple of Hera in Argos.

The subsequent history of Theseus' abduction of Hippolyta formed one of the most revealing episodes of the myth. After the abduction, Theseus took Hippolyta as his wife and she bore him a son—the Hippolytus of Euripides' tragedy. The Amazons, determined to win back their queen, invaded Attica, installed themselves on the Areopagus and elsewhere around the Akropolis, and fought a hard-pitched battle against Theseus and the Athenians.[33] In some versions, Hippolyta fought on the side of the Greeks against her own people. Another account said that she fought with the women, but in any case was killed. The Amazons were finally defeated and driven away, although their graves were pointed out to the curious in classical times and the Athenians celebrated the victory of the city over the mythical foe.

Ideas about Amazon culture were more elaborately developed than those concerning the Centaurs; the horse/men simply ate, drank, hunted in their mountains. The Amazons were said to worship Ares as well as Artemis, to be accomplished equestrians, and to love battle.[34] Unwilling to live permanently with men, they met yearly with a tribe of men to conceive children, or else took men by force. Male children they mutilated for slaves or returned to their fathers; females were raised in traditional Amazon ways, taught to ride, armed with the double-edged Amazon axe.[35] The Centaurs enacted a rejection of marriage, committing violence against it, having no need for it because they were creatures of a lost past, before sexual difference. In another way, the Amazons existed outside marriage, capable of promiscuity, seducing the Scythian men away from their wives, but also paradoxically virginal, worshipping Artemis and refusing contact with men.

Like the Centaurs, the Amazons were seen as hostile to or without need for such civilized institutions as marriage; they refused it for themselves and resisted their queen's marriage. Theirs too was imagined to be a strangely "double," hybrid culture. Their society was composed of beings who were at once feminine and masculine. They professed the activity preeminently masculine in Greek culture, the practice of war, yet paradoxically they were, like the Centaurs, a single-sex culture, one exclusively female instead of male.[36]

The monumental work of D. von Bothmer, *Amazons in Greek Art*, makes possible a consideration of the representations of the Amazons in art.[37] In a single volume, von Bothmer has collected all representations of these mythical creatures in the archaic and classical periods. Since the reader can easily refer to this text, and since in the next chapter I will treat this subject in greater depth, I here simply list certain features of representation which are relevant to an understanding of the Amazons' significance. The earlier images, especially on vases, very frequently show Amazons in combat with Herakles, presumably at their home in Themiskyra, although the city itself appears only once.[38] The invasion of Attica by the Amazons is rarely if ever shown, and the vase paintings of the Amazonomachy in Themiskyra are frequently paired with images of Herakles' other labors or at times with the Gigantomachy. Gradually, Amazons are shown in military genre scenes. In developed black-figure:

> Amazons are now shown in the same occupations as male warriors: they arm, set out for battle, return from it with their dead, lead horses, ride out, dismount, harness chariots, and drive chariots.[39]

At this stage, the Amazons wore their characteristic foreign costume, a pajama-like garment, hatched or spotted, which covered their bodies. Their skin was shown as white, in contrast against the males' in black-figure painting. The subject of Herakles and the Amazons was less frequently treated in red-figure vase painting, perhaps in part because of Herakles' association with the Athenian tyrant Peisistratos, as John Boardman has suggested.[40] The subject of the Amazonomachy, the battle between Greeks and Amazons, was still an extremely popular one. In these later works, the Amazons were often shown at ease, and their costume changed to the short belted chiton. The early classical and classical vase paintings, some of which showed extensive Amazonomachies, are associated with the appearance in Athens, in the Theseion and Peisianakteion (Stoa Poikile), of monumental Amazonomachies, created by Mikon between 460 and 438.[41] Of these paintings and of the monumental sculptural programs which included Amazonomachies more will be said later. There is an increasing practice of naming Amazons on vases in late red-figure, for example on a New York lecythos which catalogues Mimnousa, Eumache, Klymene, Hippolyte, Charope, Amynomene, Doris, and Echephyle.[42] There seems to be a shift from a focus on Hippolyta, or the all purpose "Andromache," in combat with Herakles, to a larger mass of Amazons, and an increasing focus on the Amazons as erotic objects as well, seductive perhaps because they were indeed outside the institution of marriage.

Some interpreters of the Amazon myth have attributed it to the Greeks' sighting of the beardless Hittites in an earlier period. Some, M. Zografou for example, see in the Amazons a remnant of an ancient matriarchal society, or the mythical correlate of cult practices involving armed priestesses.[43] Mandy Merck, in a recent essay, interprets the myth as an attempt by the Athenians to justify the historic claims of the patriarchal state.[44] Pierre Vidal-Naquet, in his extension of the work of Simon Pembroke, has formulated an interesting model through which one can analyze the myth of the Amazons in a less reductive way. Pembroke has shown how the ideas of Herodotos about matriarchal cultures in Asia Minor reveal a working through, by addition, subtraction, and reversal, of ideas about Greek culture—that is, Herodotos constructs a projection that inverts and alters barbarian cultures in a distorted image of their opposite, the Greek.[45] The neighboring cultures are used as alternatives through which to speculate about one's own institutions, and although Pembroke does not treat Amazon culture extensively, Herodotos' description of it in Book IV of the *Histories* falls into his categories. There Herodotos explains the history of the Amazons after their defeat by the Greeks at the river Thermodon. Carried off by the Greeks in ships, they murdered their abductors and landed in the territory of the Scythians, whose males became sexually involved with the Amazons. The Scythian men left their families and went with the Amazons to settle near Lake Maeotis. Herodotos calls the resulting group Sauromatae:

> Ever since then the women of the Sauromatae have followed their ancient usage; they ride a-hunting with their men or without them; they go to war, and wear the same dress as the men.

> The language of the Sauromatae is Scythian, but not spoken in its ancient purity, seeing that the Amazons never rightly learnt it. In regard to marriage, it is the custom that no virgin weds till she has slain a man of the enemy; and some of them grow old and die unmarried, because they cannot fulfil the law.[46]

[4.118-119]

This ethnography exhibits what Pembroke calls "reversal." The military training required of Athenian or Spartan youths at puberty, and their initiation rituals, are projected onto their opposites, the young women of the Sauromatae, descended from the

Amazons. P. Vidal-Naquet notes, in an appropriate remark, that the classical Greek *polis* was a "men's club."

> Qu'il sagisse des Amazones ou des Lyciens, la cité grecque, club d'hommes, s'est, par la voix de ses historiens et de ses "ethnographes" posée en s'opposant; Herodote apporte un admirable exemple de cette fonction d'inversion (*reversal*) quand il définit les coutumes de l'Egypte comme exactement à l'inverse de celle des Grecs (II, 35). De même, l'Etat imaginaire des Amazones est l'inverse, un inverse localisé, de la cité grecque.[47]

This insight can be developed further, beyond the ethnography of Herodotos to other manifestations of the Amazons—and the Centaurs—in the thinking of the Greeks.

In analyzing these myths, those of the Centaurs and Amazons, I have used some of the concepts of Lévi-Strauss. His notions of the nature/culture opposition, his description of such institutions as "the exchange of women," illuminate certain habits of mind of the Greeks. They also lead directly to the ways in which the myths of the Centaurs and the Amazons, and their representations on works of art, are relevant to a study of difference in the classical period. The myths work out, in narrative form, certain notions of the founding of culture and the defining of boundaries of culture.

The Elementary Structures of Kinship, first published in 1949, is not at present a text in vogue, yet it is relevant to my purpose in spite of criticisms levelled at it by anthropologists.[48] It is useful partly because it betrays a bias about human culture which the Greeks shared. Lévi-Strauss claims in this work that human culture is founded on the incest taboo, on exogamy, on the "exchange of women." Anthropologists working in specific fields have challenged the details of this study; in a sense its inaccuracies in terms of ethnology make it all the more valuable as a created structure through which men see history, a myth like those of the Greeks.[49]

The Greeks shared some of Lévi-Strauss' assumptions about culture, about the significant form of marriage patterns in determining the boundaries of social life. Propositions about Amazons and Centaurs, for example, are part of a system of speculation concerning exogamy and endogamy, and they thus implicitly define difference for Greek culture. Like the Greeks, Lévi-Strauss tries, in *The Elementary Structures* and elsewhere, to see women as tokens, things to be exchanged by men, "words" in a conversation that founds culture.[50] He says:

> The law of exogamy . . . is omnipresent, acting permanently and continually; moreover—it applies to valuables, *viz.*, women—valuables *par excellence* from both the biological and social points of view. . . .[51]

Exogamy defines the group and it also defines other groups in the "marital dialogue"—those excluded from relations of exchange are "other." Lévi-Strauss thus describes what he calls "true endogamy":

> . . . marriage rules do not always merely prohibit a kinship circle, but occasionally also fix one within which marriage must necessarily take place, under pain of the same scandal as would result if the prohibition itself were violated. There are two cases to be distinguished here: on the one hand endogamy, or the obligation to marry within an objectively defined group; and on the other, preferential union or the obligation to choose as spouse an individual who is related to Ego in some particular way. . . . True endogamy is merely the refusal to recognize the possibility of marriage beyond the limits of the human community. The definitions of this community are many and varied, depending on the philosophy of the group considered. A very great number of primitive tribes simply refer to themselves by the term for "men" in their language, showing that in their eyes an essential characteristic of man disappears outside the limits of the group.[52]

The Greeks' early speculation about culture, about boundaries, shares such characteristics. Those excluded from marriage are excluded from culture. It is this fact which makes Lévi-Strauss' formulations so useful for the Greek material. Julian Pitt-Rivers has recently demonstrated, in a study of "honor" in the Mediterranean, that

> ... Mediterranean endogamy is, rather than a rule forbidding marriage outside a given social range, a preference for keeping daughters as close to the nuclear family as the prohibition of incest permits.[53]

These ideas about endogamy are not universal, even in the Mediterranean. Nonetheless, they are particularly appropriate for the period of the classical city, when the project of defining the boundaries of social life was all-important.[54] Restrictions enforcing endogamy were common practice; in 451 Pericles passed a law in Athens requiring that any citizen have two citizen parents, and this law, which fell into disuse in the Peloponnesian War, was reiterated after the war.[55]

In an important discussion in the *Politics*, Aristotle reveals how ideas of marriage and endogamy were crucial in defining the limits of the *polis*:

> And if one were actually to bring the sites of two cities together into one, so that the city-walls of Megara and those of Corinth were contiguous, even so they would not be one city, [*ou mia polis*] nor would they if they enacted rights of intermarriage [*epigamias*] with one another, although intermarriage between citizens is one of the elements of community which are characteristic of states.
>
> [*Politics* 1280b10-15][56]

Epigamia, intermarriage, is seen as a crucial though not sufficient condition for the community of a *polis*.

Aristotle's speculation about the nature of the *polis* was preceded in the fifth century by mythic speculation about boundaries, and the myths of the Amazons and Centaurs constitute part of this inquiry. Both myths touch on the limits of culture and use marriage as a model for culture. As I argued earlier, the Centaurs represent the negation of marriage for the Greeks, and all the episodes of the myth concerning Ixion reveal this role. Even the episodes recounted of Herakles show the Centaurs hostile to relations of exchange—their refusal to share wine with Herakles is equivalent to their attempt to take the Lapith women through rape. The notion of commensality, discussed by Pitt-Rivers, is structurally parallel to endogamy: cultures which share food share women.[57] The Centaurs violated the rules of exchange by denying food and then attempting to "consume" human women. In the episodes of Peirithoös' wedding feast and of Nessos' attempt to rape Deianeira, the social consequences of the Centaurs' bestiality were played out.

The Amazons too can be seen as mythical creatures hostile to marriage. Their very society denied the necessity of marriage. Men were used by them for reproduction, but their domestic life was predicated on exclusion. The myths told of them were significantly parallel to those concerning the Centaurs. In the episode of Herakles and his labors—the gaining of the girdle of Hippolyta—the Greek hero invaded the territory of the Amazons, just as he invaded the Centaurs' space on Mount Pholoe. Herakles' acquisition of the girdle is structurally parallel to his insistence on drinking the wine of the Centaurs. The loosening of the girdle was the traditional euphemism for the loss of virginity among the Greeks; marriage was the acceptable form of that loosening. Herakles' invasion of the Amazons represented a metaphorical rape of Amazon culture. The subsequent episodes of the Amazon myth, those concerning Theseus, touched even more explicitly on the theme of marriage. Theseus' abduction of the Amazon queen represented a rectification of their attitude towards exchange. What would not be exchanged would be seized. The Amazons' invasion of Attica clearly showed their hostility to the institution of marriage, and was structurally similar to the Centaurs' disruption of Peirithoös' wedding. The Amazons were consistently anti-marriage figures; the fate of Hippolytus in Euripides' tragedy was the inevitable consequence of a male child's being born to a union between Greek and Amazon in marriage.[58] Once Theseus and Hippolyta were united, the Amazons' invasion and attempt to restore Hippolyta to them were consistent with their violations of marriage practice. They expected to return her to their single-sex culture, in which social marriage was impossible, where male children were killed, mutilated, or returned to the tribe of their fathers. The death of the queen was the result.

Both series of myths reveal creatures at the boundaries of culture, whose imagined societies had limited resources for reproduction, but which represented distorted alternatives to the culture of the Greeks in which intermarriage was the norm.

Marriage, that is, in Lévi-Strauss' sense, the exchange of women between men of the same kind, was culture for the Greeks. Herodotos' evidence on this question is revealing, not only in the passages in his text where he comments on marriage among the barbarians. At the very beginning of the *Histories*, he discusses women-stealing in terms which illustrate Greek thinking about endogamy. He traces the origin of the hostilities between Greeks and barbarians to woman-stealing. The Phoenicians stole Io, the Greeks carried off Europa, then Medea, and Paris took Helen.

> Thus far it was a matter of mere robbery [*harpagas*] on both sides. But after this (the Persians say) the Greeks were greatly to blame; for they invaded Asia before the Persians attacked Europe. "We think," say they, "that it is wrong to carry women off [*harpazein gunaikas*]: but to be zealous to avenge the rape is foolish: wise men take no account of such things: for plainly the women would never have been carried away, had not they themselves wished it. We of Asia regarded the rape of our women not at all; but the Greeks, all for the sake of a Lacedaemonian woman, mustered a great host, came to Asia, and destroyed the power of Priam. Ever since then we have regarded Greeks as our enemies." The Persians claim Asia for their own, and the foreign nations that dwell in it; Europe and the Greek race they hold to be separate from them [*kechôristhai*].
>
> [1.4]

Herodotos displaces the observation about the Greeks onto the Persians, yet the judgement indicates the stress the Greeks laid on questions of the exchange of women, and the power of endogamy to describe boundaries of difference.[59] From the beginning the model of the Trojan War, the defining historical myth of the

Greeks, established their separateness by means of exclusiveness in the exchange of women. The Greeks saw themselves as a single culture, defined by an *internal* process of exchange; exchange or theft across those boundaries was theoretically a violation of their autonomous culture and cause for war. The traditional, long-enduring division of mankind into Greeks and barbarians is here justified by Herodotos purely in terms of differing attitudes about 'marriage,' that is, about the relations among men in their exchange of women.

The myths of Centaurs and Amazons were used by the Greeks to reflect on the institution of marriage and on exchange as a cultural practice. As I will show in the next chapter, the representation of these mythical beings in art, linked by analogy with animals, with barbarians, with women, reveals the nature of their concern about community and its limits, about difference.

NOTES

1. See n. 41 of introduction.

2. On the pre-Socratics, see W.K.C. Guthrie, *A History of Greek Philosophy* (Cambridge, 1962-1975), vols. 1, 2. G.S. Kirk and J.E. Raven, *The Presocratic Philosophers*, (Cambridge, 1957); Havelock, *The Liberal Temper.* Important recent work on Heraclitus includes Jean Bollack and Henri Wismann, *Héraclite, ou la séparation* (Paris, 1972); Charles Kahn, *The Art and Thought of Heraclitus* (Cambridge, 1979).

3. *The Odes of Pindar*, with English translation by J. Sandys, rev. ed. (Cambridge, Mass. and London [Loeb] 1937). Translation slightly modified. See Charles Segal, "God and Man in Pindar's First and Third Olympian Odes," *HSCP* 68 (1964): 211-67.

4. See Claude Lévi-Strauss, "The Structural Study of Myth in *Structural Anthropology*, trans. by C. Jacobson and B.G. Schoepf (Garden City, N.Y., 1967), pp. 202-28.

5. On Kassite boundary stones, see *Cambridge Ancient History* vol. 2, part 2, 3rd edition (Cambridge, 1975), p. 46.

6. Pindar, *Pythian* 2, 21 ff. with scholia. Aeschylus, fragments of *Ixion* and *Perrhaibides.*

7. Marcel Detienne, *The Gardens of Adonis*, trans. by J. Lloyd (Atlantic Highlands, New Jersey, 1977), first pub. as *Les jardins d'Adonis* (Paris, 1972).

8. Pindar, *Pythian* 2. 31 ff.

9. See Scholiast at Apollonius Rhodius, *Argonautica*, 3.62, quoting Pherecydes.

10. Pindar, *Pythian* 2. 44.

11. Detienne, op. cit.

12. Apollodorus, 2. 83 ff.

13. G.S. Kirk, *Myth, Its Meanings and Functions in Ancient and Other Cultures* (Berkeley and Los Angeles, 1970), pp. 152-62. See also Charles Segal, "The Raw and the Cooked in Greek Literature: Structure, Values, Metaphor," *CJ* 69:4 (1974): 289-300.

14. Homer, *Iliad* 1. 262 ff.; 2. 742; 14. 317 ff.; and *Odyssey* 21. 295 ff.; ps.-Hesiod, *Shield*, 178 ff.; Pindar, frag. 167 (Bergk); Apollonius Rhodius, 1. 57 ff.; Ovid, *Met.* 12. 182 ff.

15. Hesiod, frag. 96, 49 ff.

16. Hesiod, *Theogony*, 1002; Apollonius Rhodius 2. 1231 ff., and schol.

17. Paul V.C. Baur, *Centaurs in Ancient Art, The Archaic Period* (Berlin, 1912).

18. Ibid., p. 78.

19. Ibid., p. 100.

20. Georges Dumézil, *Le Problème des Centaures. Etude de mythologie comparée indo-européenne* (Paris, 1929), p. 257.

21. Jeffrey Henderson, *The Maculate Muse: Obscene Language in Attic Comedy* (New Haven and London, 1975), p. 122.

22. Ibid., p. 127.

23. Ibid., p. 133.

24. Ibid., pp. 178-79.

25. Ibid., pp. 202-3, 219.

26. Baur, op. cit., p. 119. But see, for example, the Gorgon as Centauress on a Boeotian pithos now in the Louvre (CA 795).

27. B.B. Shefton, "Herakles and Theseus on a Red-Figured Louterion," *Hesp.* 31 (1962): 330-68.

28. On the Amazon myth, see Donald J. Sobol, *The Amazons of Greek Mythology* (South Brunswick and New York, 1972) who argues: "In all, the lesson embodied (in the myth) was that Amazonian aggressions could be thwarted by using resourcefulness rather than crude strength." [90]; G.C. Rothery, *The Amazons in Antiquity and Modern Times* (London, 1910); Pierre Samuel, *Amazones, guerrières et gaillardes* (Grenoble, 1975).

29.   Homer, *Iliad* 6. 155 ff.; Plutarch, *On Virtue of Women.*

30.   Vergil, *Aeneid* 1. 490 ff.; Quintus Smyrnaeus, *Post-Homerica* 1. 538-810. See Proclus on Arktinos of Miletus.

31.   Apollonius Rhodius 2. 966 ff. Apollodorus 2., 98 ff.

32.   Plutarch, *Life of Theseus,* 24 ff.; Herodotos 9.27.4.

33.   See for many citations, W.R. Halliday, *The Greek Questions of Plutarch* (London, 1928), 209 ff.

34.   See Florence Mary Bennett, *Religious Cults Associated with the Amazons* (New York, 1967), p. 18.

35.   Diodorus Siculus 3. 69-70.

36.   See J.J. Bachofen, *Myth, Religion, and Mother Right,* trans. by R. Manheim (Princeton, 1967), on "Amazonism," the extreme form of the matriarchal stage of human evolution, pp. 104-6.

37.   Dietrich von Bothmer, *Amazons in Greek Art* (Oxford, 1957).

38.   Ibid., pl. 10 (Florence 3773).

39.   Ibid., p. 91.

40.   John Boardman, "Herakles, Peisistratos and Eleusis," *JHS* 45 (1975): 1-2, and "Herakles, Peisistratos and Sons," *Revue Archéologique* I (1972): 62.

41.   Ibid., p. 200; Lucy Shoe Meritt, "The Stoa Poikile," *Hesp.* 39 (1970): 233-64; J.P. Barron, "New Light on Old Walls: The Murals of the Theseion," *JHS* 42 (1972): 20-45, which contains a good survey of the iconography concerning Centaurs and Amazons.

42.   von Bothmer, op. cit., pl. 77.1 (New York 31.11.13), discussed on page 173. See Bennett, op. cit., pp. 75-76.

43.   M. Zografou, *Amazons in Homer and Hesiod. A Historical Reconstruction* (Athens, 1972).

44.   The Amazons, I would argue, are not introduced into myth as an independent force, but as the vanquished opponents of heroes credited with the establishment and protection of the Athenian state, its founding fathers, so to speak. Patriotism reinforces patriarchalism to define the tribeswomen as opponents of the state, an image potent enough to be invoked by aspirant politicians.

Mandy Merck, "The City's Achievements, the Patriotic Amazonomachy and Ancient Athens," in *Tearing the Veil,* ed. by Susan Lipschitz (London, 1978), p. 96.

45.   Simon Pembroke, "Women in Charge: The Function of Alternatives in Early Greek Tradition and the Ancient Idea of Matriarchy," *JWCI* 30 (1967): 1-35, and "Last of the Matriarchs:

A Study in the Inscriptions of Lycia," *Journal of the Economic and Social History of the Orient* 8:3 (1965): 217-47; see also Joan Bamberger, "The Myth of Matriarchy: Why Men Rule in Primitive Society," in *Woman, Culture, and Society*, ed. by M.Z. Rosaldo and L. Lamphere (Stanford, 1974). Pembroke argues, for example, in "Last of the Matriarchs . . . ," that the Greek inscriptions in Lycia, as well as Lycian texts, substantiate a family structure far closer to that of Greece than Herodotos' account indicates.

46. Herodotus, *Histories*, with an English trans. by A.D. Godley, 4 vols. (Cambridge, Mass., and London [Loeb], 1926); on the Amazon invasion of Attica, 9.27. See also A.O. Lovejoy and George Boas, *Primitivism and Related Ideas in Antiquity* (New York, 1965), pp. 288 ff.

47. P. Vidal-Naquet, "Esclavage et gynécocratie dans la tradition, le mythe, l'utopie," in *Recherches sur les structures sociales dans l'antiquité* (Actes du Colloque de Caen) (Paris, 1970), pp. 63-80.

48. Claude Lévi-Strauss, *The Elementary Structures of Kinship*, trans. by J.H. Bell, J.R. von Sturmer, and R. Needham, ed., rev. ed. (Boston, 1969), first pub. as *Les structures élémentaires de la parenté* (Paris, 1949). See, for example, Lévi-Strauss' answer to some critics in his preface to the second edition of *Elementary Structures*, written in 1966.

49. See, among others, Pierre Bourdieu, *Outline of a Theory of Practice*, trans. by R. Nice (Cambridge, 1977), which contains a detailed summary of "the state of the question" of parallel cousin marriage, pp. 32-33. He argues:

> Matrimonial strategies, objectively directed towards the conservation or expansion of the material and symbolic capital jointly possessed by a more or less extended group, belong to the system of reproduction strategies, defined as the sum total of the strategies through which individuals or groups objectively tend to reproduce the relations of production associated with a determinate mode of production by striving to reproduce or improve their position in the social structure.

> This takes us a long way from the pure—because infinitely impoverished—realm of the "rules of marriage" and the "elementary structures of kinship."
>
> [70]

50. Lévi-Strauss says, in *Structural Anthropology*, defending himself:

... these results (analysis of kinship) can be achieved only by treating marriage regulations as a kind of language, a set of processes permitting the establishment, between individuals and groups, of a certain type of communication. That the mediating factor, in this case, should be the *women of the group*, who are *circulated* between clans, lineages, or families, in place of the *words of the group*, which are *circulated* between individuals, does not at all change the fact that the essential aspect of the phenomenon is identical in both cases. . . . Women are held by the social group to be values of the most essential kind, though we have difficulty in understanding how these values become integrated in systems endowed with a significant function. This ambiguity is clearly manifested in the reactions of persons who on the basis of the analysis of social structures referred to, have laid against it the charge of 'anti-feminism', because women are referred to as objects. Of course, it may be disturbing to some to have women conceived as mere parts of a meaningful system. . . .

"Language and the Analysis of Social Laws," in *Structural Anthropology*, p. 60. Lévi-Strauss goes on to concede that women cannot be reduced to pure signs, since they can speak. Later in the same text, in a discussion of social structure, he says "In any society, communication operates on three different levels: communication of women, communication of goods and services, communication of messages" [289].

51.   Lévi-Strauss, *Elementary Structures*, p. 481.

52.   Ibid., 45-46.

53.   Julian Pitt-Rivers, *The Fate of Shechem or the Politics of Sex, Essays in the Anthropology of the Mediterranean* (Cambridge, 1977), p. 162.

54.   The creation of this idea of the city, as a circle of equals united spatially around a common hearth, and in terms of common interests, is usually attributed to the reforms of the sixth century. In its last years, the Athenian Cleisthenes altered the electoral system of the *polis*, replacing tribal affiliations with other ties. The *dêmos* became the basic unit of the city, and the old groups (clan and phratry) could no longer control the *polis*. Cleisthenes also grouped the demes of the three geographical areas of the city, the town, coast, and interior, into *trittyes*, so that no single geographical area could dominate. According to N.G.L. Hammond:

The electoral system gave to all Athenians, regardless of birth or wealth, an equality of political rights in the election of local and state officials. . . . As distinct from a tyranny or a close oligarchy (*dynasteia*), the Athenian state was described as an equality in rights, in speech, or in power (*isonomia*, *isegoria*, or *isokratia*).

A History of Greece to 322 B.C., 2nd ed. (Oxford, 1967), p. 190. Aristotle describes the process in the *Constitution of Athens*, 21-22.

Vernant discusses the reforms of Cleisthenes in a review of the work of P. Leveque and P. Vidal-Naquet on this period (*Mythe et pensée*, 207 ff.). In an essay entitled "Géometrie et astronomie sphérique dans la première cosmologie grecque," *Mythe et pensée*, 171 ff. he describes the *polis* as a structure analogous to that of the circular cosmology of Anaximander. Already in the sixth century the city began to be thought of as a circle of equals:

Dans ce centre chacun se trouve l'égal l'un de l'autre, personne n'est soumise à personne. Dans ce libre débat qui s'institue au centre de l'*agora*, tous les citoyens se définissent comme de *isoi*, des égaux, des *homoioi*, des semblables. Nous voyons naître une société où le rapport de l'homme avec l'homme est pensé sous la forme d'une relation d'identité, de symétrie, de réversibilité.

[154]

The city's idea of itself as a circle of equals intensifies in the fifth century. Although women, slaves, and metics are excluded from electoral privileges, within the circle of citizenship the body of equals, male, Greek, human, see inside the boundaries of the city a society of identity. Emile Benveniste, in differentiating between Greek and Roman ideas of the city, characterizes the Greek *polis* as "corps abstrait, état, source et centre de l'autorité," op. cit., vol. 2, p. 278.

55. Hammond, op. cit., pp. 301 and 447. See also Aristotle, *Ath.* 26.3.

56. Aristotle, *Politics*, with trans. by H. Rackham (London and Cambridge Mass., [Loeb], 1932).

57. Pitt-Rivers, op. cit., pp. 124-25.

58. See also Aeschylus, *Suppliants* 277-290, where the Danaids are compared to Amazons; *Eumenides* 628, as Apollo accuses Clytemnestra, and 685-690, Athena on the Areopagus and the Amazon invasion.

59. On Herodotus, see M. Rosellini and S. Saïd, "Usages de femmes et autres nomoi chez les 'sauvages' d'Hérodote: Essai de lecture structurale," in *Annali della scuola normale superiore di Pisa*,

(Classe di lettere e filosofia) 8:3 (1978): 949-1005; and François Hartog, *Le Miroir d'Hérodote* (Paris, 1980), especially pp. 229-37 on the Amazons.

II

Centauromachy/Amazonomachy

The last chapter showed how the myths of Amazons and Centaurs were seen to be implicated, in Greek culture, in a pattern of speculation about endogamy, marriage, and exchange, with notions of boundaries defining a norm. This chapter will elaborate these themes, in particular focusing on the representations of Amazons and Centaurs in works of art of the fifth century, both to demonstrate how the themes are explicated and to establish further categories of analysis. Myth, and the works of art which figure forth myth, participate in the project of the culture, the implicit differentiation of kinds, the centering on the Greek male citizen.

Before considering the representations of Amazons and Centaurs in art, however, it would be appropriate to describe the type of analysis that follows. Erwin Panofsky, in his programmatic essay "Iconography and Iconology," discussed the ideal relationship between three separate phases of cultural history—the "pre-iconographical description," the iconographical analysis, and iconological interpretation.[1] The pre-iconographical description involves the history of style, the iconographical analysis the history of types. Both these kinds of study are exemplified by Dietrich von Bothmer's impressive work *Amazons in Greek Art.* The third stratum of analysis, the iconological, involves what Panofsky calls "history of *cultural symptoms* or *'symbols'* in general (insight into the manner in which, under varying historical conditions, *essential tendencies of the human mind* were expressed by specific *themes* and *concepts).*"[2] Without accepting unquestioningly Panofsky's belief in "essential tendencies of the human mind," I am concerned here with the specific tendency of the Greeks to define themselves in terms of difference, and with the specific elements with which this theme was expressed in the classical age.

49

The Greeks used the myth of the Amazons as well as that of the Centaurs to work out and represent a program of differentiation through polarity and analogy. My "iconological" study of their representation in works of art depends on the iconographical studies of von Bothmer, Baur, and others.[3]

Included in the iconological interpretation must be a consideration of formal aspects of the iconography concerned, not simply an analysis of content. In this sense, classical art historians have for the most part avoided an "iconological" analysis, in that they discuss changes in form most frequently in terms of an evolutionary model which finds the origins of Greek art in Egypt, Crete, and Mesopotamia, goes on to trace the rise of naturalistic representation, and points finally to a decadence of form in Hellenistic art.[4] To perform an analysis of art as a phenomenon within its culture, it is necessary not only to do an iconological interpretation, but also to consider formal changes in their historical context. Classical art historians have tended to consider these features in isolation, in terms of the autonomous development of techniques of representation.

Yet formal relationships are extremely revealing. For example, on a black-figure eye cup in the British Museum,[5] the Amazonomachy and Geryonomachy appear on opposite sides; von Bothmer remarks on the suggestive sharing of motifs:

> . . . one is tempted to see in the pair of defending Amazons next to the body of the fallen Andromache an adaptation of the familiar tricorporeal Geryon. This adaptation, or perhaps assimilation, becomes more apparent in the contemporary red-figured Amazonomachy by the Andokides Painter . . . and, a little later, in the Amazonomachies by Euphronios . . .[6]

This resemblance is not accidental, nor should it be attributed simply to formal convenience. In one version of the Herakles myth, Geryon dwelt in the Far West, near the sunset and the entrance to Hades, and to reach him Herakles sailed in the sun's golden cup. He then killed Geryon and took his cattle. In Herodotos' account of the Geryon labor, the hero returned through Scythia from Geryon's home (IV, 8-10), and there encountered "a viper-woman—a creature which from the buttocks upwards was a woman, but below them was a snake." She kept Herakles with her until she bore him three sons, one of whom was the eponymous hero of the Scythians, Scythes, thus the supposed ancestor of the Sauromatae. The episodes of the myth treat of hybrid monsters in all cases, and with dangerous women who survive without men, needing them only for reproduction. The content of the mythic nexus is intriguing, and includes Herakles' enslavement to Omphale. At present I am concerned only to point out the way in which formal aspects of the cup, the tricorporeality of the monster Geryon, Herakles' opponent, and his "human" opponents' tri-corporeality, reinforce the attribution of monstrosity to the Amazons. The kinds of beings on this black-figure cup are made analogous through the artist's formal opposition of them.[7]

The formal analogy is made, perhaps accidentally by the painter, more deliberately by the inventor of the sculptural program of such a massive work as the Athenian treasury at Delphi, where Theseus and Herakles are carefully "opposed." The principles of form—juxtaposition, opposition, framing—have perhaps been insufficiently discussed by art historians of the classical period, although in other fields formal relationship has been considered an important clue to relationships of a more conceptual nature.[8]

The manner in which the formal concepts are used in representation is peculiar to classical art and its imitations. The first notion is that of analogy, mentioned above, in which one model, one concept is used to illuminate another. In the particular case of classical art, the use of analogy can take the form of the example discussed above, where the representation of the Amazons is formally analogous to the traditional representation of the Geryonomachy. The formal relationship between the two motifs sets up an analogical relationship between Amazons and Geryon, and an equivalence is thus established between these two traditional opponents of the Greek hero. Juxtaposition is another way in which such forms can be linked; two figures, two scenes, two episodes from myth can be placed next to each other on a work of art and thus made equivalent, or related by a logical procedure which presents them as contraries rather than equals.

Opposition in formal terms is similar to juxtaposition; by this I mean simply that on a work of art such as a Greek vase the reverse and obverse of the vase may bear representations which have a relationship to one another. Even though the coupling of subjects on the vases was fixed by tradition, and was subject to the tastes of the individual artists, the very fact that two subjects were understood properly to be opposed to one another in this way is significant and revealing about processes of thought. In the archaic, transitional, and earlier red-figure periods, for example, vases usually bore two central mythological scenes, one each on obverse and reverse. Later in the fifth century, painters began to use one side of the vase more frequently for scenes of daily life—erotic scenes, youths and women together, scenes of drinking and feasting.[9] The change is part of the aesthetic crisis I mentioned above, a crisis which led to a shift away from mythic thinking toward a focus on the present, on life in the *polis.* The juxtaposition of a contemporary drinking party with a Dionysiac procession, for example, assimilates the mythic reality to the experience of daily life in the city. The very shapes of Greek vases, as of coins and architectural decoration, in the classical period especially, were appropriate to this type of paired, always symmetrical relationship among representations. The Greeks' fondness for symmetry, for objects which permit this type of balancing and opposition, is expressed also in their modes of reasoning, through polarizing and analogizing. The sprawling octopi of Minoan vases, for example, correspond to a radically different scheme for ordering reality.[10]

In his work on the Hestia-Hermes opposition in Greek ideas of space and movement, J.-P. Vernant demonstrates how the principle of symmetry worked.[11] Hestia represents a fixed central space, in the city and in the home, and Hermes the very idea of change and mobility around the center.[12] To clarify the opposition between the two, Vernant notes that Pheidias showed the gods Hestia and Hermes together in the pairings of the twelve gods on the base of the great statue of Zeus at Olympia (Pausanias 3.11.3).[13] Their juxtaposition reveals their affinity of function in religious thought; it marks as well their analogical relationship to the other couples thus shown—Zeus-Hera, Poseidon-Amphitrite, and others—as man and wife, brother and sister, mother and son, etc. Such formal placement is clearly not arbitrary. The two logical types of similarity and opposition are characteristic of what Lévy-Bruhl called the "pre-logical mentality," but which G.E.R. Lloyd prefers to call the "informal logic implicit in primitive or archaic thought."[14] This logic which the Greeks used in the classical period, that of analogy and polarity, was expressed in artistic as well as literary texts.

The juxtaposition of the Amazonomachy and Centauromachy in the artistic production of the fifth century B.C. is an example of this logic. Through this juxtaposition, the myths came to carry a certain burden of speculation about difference for the Greeks. G.S. Kirk, in *Myth, Its Meanings and Functions in Ancient and Other Cultures*, links the Centaurs not with the Amazons but with the Cyclopes. He points out correspondences between them, then remarks:

> These correspondences . . . are hardly deliberate. They are neither emphasized in the way in which deliberate correspondences were, nor marked by cross-references between the two groups, nor noticed by ancient mythographers still in touch, even if indirectly, with the oral tradition.[15]

The correspondences between Centaurs and Amazons *were*, on the other hand, strongly stressed by ancient artists, and by the architects who planned the sculptural programs of monumental civic buildings in the fifth century. For this reason alone, it seems important to consider the ways in which these myths are related. One of the difficulties of a Lévi-Straussian approach to myth—like Kirk's—is that it fails to take into account the ways in which literate cultures use and elaborate myth.[16] Although Lévi-Strauss claims, for example, to have analyzed all versions of the Oedipus myth, including Freud's, in a famous essay to which classicists frequently allude, his analysis is extremely unconvincing.[17] A text like Sophocles' *Oedipus Rex* is part of a historical moment, and the particular shaping by the tragedian of mythic material cannot be accounted for satisfactorily by an ahistorical structuralism.

As many critics have noted, the Amazonomachy and the Centauromachy were frequently juxtaposed on works of art in the fifth century, sometimes with the Gigantomachy.[18] In fact, the first object listed by von Bothmer as depicting an Amazon, a terra-cotta votive shield from Tiryns dated from the turn of the eighth century, shows a Centaur as well.[19] Again and again, the battle between Lapiths and Centaurs, the battle between Greeks and Amazons, appear together in the mythic programs of the classical city. Bernard Ashmole calls them "tedious subjects," and accounts for the persistence of the juxtaposition thus: the "white bodies of Amazons against brown bodies of Greeks" . . . afforded "a piquant contrast which must, I fear, have contributed to the popularity of the subject."[20] Although the contrast he remarks is significant, his disinterest in these subjects seems strangely ethnocentric. The very popularity of these themes, and their frequent repetition in art, show that they treated issues of concern to those who made art in the city.

Other scholars have commented that the persistence of the theme is due to an interest in the female body; since Greek women were never represented in violent movement, the Amazons alone afforded an opportunity for the artist to represent the female body in action.[21] Another traditional reading of the Amazonomachy/Centauromachy theme, an attempt to explain its great popularity in the fifth century, is that it provides the artist with a way of showing allegorically the invasion of the Persians, and their defeat by the Greeks, at the beginning of the fifth century.[22]

In this reading of the works of art on which they are juxtaposed, or opposed, the Centaurs and Amazons represent allegorically the army of barbarians, led by Darius and then by Xerxes. One of the interesting problems of the fifth century is the prohibition against direct representation of historical subjects in art and in literature; this is a question which will be taken up further in my discussion of the *Persae*. One of the few works of art in the classical city on which the Persians were represented directly was the Stoa Poikile (460), which had paintings showing the battle of Marathon as well as Theseus engaged in the Amazonomachy in Attica, according to Pausanias' *ekphrasis*. On most works of art of the fifth century, however, the Persians were shown allegorically, very often through the figures of Centaurs and Amazons.

As Roger Hinks pointed out in *Myth and Allegory in Ancient Art*, the Greeks avoided direct narrative representation of the events of history. The Athenian "preferred to conceal his memory of the great ordeal of Marathon and Thermopylae and Salamis" through the "mythical transposition of historical episodes."[23] Hinks would deny the appellation allegory to the Amazonomachy, since the narrative structure of the artistic text does not correspond to the metaphorical intention: in his vocabulary, the relations between symbols must "mean," if true allegory is present.[24] In the Amazonomachy, he sees only the fact of battle, and thus only "myth." The specific historical event is treated as a "symbolic situation" through allusion to the "moral conflict of which the political clash is the outward and contingent expression."[25] The work of art simply gives particular form to the general idea, and with this view of the Amazonomachy Bruno Snell concurs:

> For the Greeks, the Titanomachy and the battle against the giants remained symbols of the victory which their own world had won over a strange universe; along with the battles against the Amazons and Centaurs they continue to signalize the Greek conquest of everything barbarous, of all monstrosity and grossness.[26]

Thus the Persian War itself simply exemplifies a general principle of the cosmos, the superiority of the Greeks to barbarians. Amazons and Centaurs therefore represent barbarism, and chaos.

Nevertheless, the specific historical reference can be followed through in more detail in the works of art, even though what Hinks would call allegory may not appear. Thus even the simple equation between Amazons and Centaurs and Persians can be elaborated and deepened through an examination of the historical context. Anthony Podlecki, in his study of the political background of Aeschylean tragedy, has remarked that painters and sculptors celebrated various figures of the period of the Persian wars:

> There is a convergence of scattered lines of evidence to show that in the decade after 480 a controversy arose over which victory over the Persians—Marathon or Salamis—was the most important. A propaganda battle seems to have developed between Cimon, whose father Miltiades had been

the hero of Marathon, and Themistocles, author of the victory of Salamis. Each side enlisted the help not only of poets, but also of painters and sculptors, to impress its own version of the facts on public opinion.[27]

Podlecki establishes links among Cimon, the painter Polygnotus, who painted the Amazonomachy in the Stoa Poikile, and the hero Theseus who was said to have appeared to aid the Greeks at Marathon. He argues that Cimon was making an analogy between Miltiades and Theseus in order to advance his own political career, to represent himself as another analogue of Theseus.

This sort of direct allusion to contemporary events within works of art suggests that much more can be done with an analysis of artistic evidence, even at the simplest level of an analogy between Centaurs and Amazons and the Persians. In the works of art, the naked bodies of the Greek and Lapith soldiers, set against the chaotic hybrid disorder of the Centaurs and the unnatural violence of the Amazons, showed the real character of the Persian threat and established the contemporary Greek heroes as the analogical equivalents of the legendary heroes of the past.

The conclusions reached in the last chapter concerning the myths told of these creatures can also be applied to their representation in art. The Centaurs and Amazons—violators of human culture, foreign to proper exchange, anti-marriage—are drawn into the characterization of the Persians through patterns of polarizing and analogical reasoning. The Persians, like the mythical beings who stand for them, violated patterns of giving and receiving which founded human culture. They demanded earth and water from the Greeks without respecting the limits of difference. They are represented as asymmetrical, imbalanced societies, marked like the over-masculine or over-feminized societies of Amazons and Centaurs as defective, uncivilized, at once seductive and menacing, a threat to the human institutions of exchange and endogamy, and thus to human culture in general. The specific characteristics of the Persians were thus made analogous to those of Amazons and Centaurs. They were seen as violators of all civilized norms, to be excluded from relations of reciprocity.

The analogy between Centaurs and Amazons and Persians is the most prominent and the most historically specific of the analogies made in the repeated representations of these mythic battles in fifth century art. There are other elements, however, which emerge from a careful reading of these motifs, other ways in which speculation concerning difference occurs, which situate the comparison between Greeks and barbarians in a larger pattern of differentiation. Before going into these questions, which involve not narrative analysis but an exacting interrogation of myth and art in their formal patternings, I want to trace the Amazonomachy/Centauromachy on several monuments of the late sixth and early fifth centuries.

The first of these works of art, a transitional work containing the Amazonomachy alone, was probably constructed before the Persian Wars, although the dating is disputed. The excavators of the Athenian treasury at Delphi follow Pausanias in ascribing the building of the treasury to the period after the victory at Marathon;[28] Pausanias says the edifice was constructed with the battle spoils (10.11.5). Von Bothmer, following Dinsmoor and others, supports instead a date in the last decade of the sixth century.[29] The treasury, a beautiful, compact building, originally had thirty metopes; the exploits of Herakles were represented on the north side, on the west appeared the Geryonomachy, on the East the Amazonomachy, and on the south the exploits of Theseus.

This elaborate artistic text forms a crucial first moment in the pattern to be discussed, the working out of differentiation among kinds, in that it operates a transposition of the myth of the Amazons from the myths concerning Herakles to those which center on Theseus. This supposed founder of the *polis* of Athena effected the *synoikismos*, the association of the people of Attica into a political unit surrounding Athens.[30] The shifting of mythic material has frequently been noted; Karl Galinsky has shown that throughout the myths about Theseus there was an attempt to model his achievements on those of Herakles.[31] Some scholars have stressed the affiliations between Herakles and the tyrant Peisistratos, while C.M. Bowra offers another suggestion about the transformation of the myths. Herakles was "almost the ideal embodiment of the Greek settler, who destroyed aboriginal monsters and gave peace to the regions which he traversed."[32]

Herakles, who in archaic art is often shown clothed in the lion's skin, his head emerging from the beast's mouth, had

affinities with the monsters he encountered. His violent history
served as a model of colonization, mythically recounting his
adventures as he moved from the western to the eastern boundaries of the world, exterminating creatures who stood in the way
of the civilizing presence of the Greeks. He was the cleanser, the
hero who could not really be tolerated within the city because of
his bestiality, his crudity, his violence.[33] Theseus, on the other
hand, was a man of the *polis*, a beautiful, graceful youth. Martin
Nilsson remarks that he was "the Athenian youth educated in the
palaestra . . ."; while Herakles killed ferocious beasts, Theseus
conquered highwaymen and robbers, "enemies of a peaceful and
civilized life."[34]

The Athenian treasury at Delphi enacts the transformation of
the Amazonomachy from Herakles to Theseus. If von Bothmer is
correct, and the Amazonomachy there represents the episode of
Herakles' battle at Themiskyra to gain the girdle of Hippolyta,
with Theseus as his companion, the work of art serves to associate
the two heroes by analogy and in effect to transfer the power of
the Amazon defeater away from the archaic hero Herakles to the
Athenian Theseus. If Geryon is Herakles' enemy, then the Amazons are Theseus'. If both Theseus and Herakles participate in
the battle of Themiskyra, while the west side metopes show
Herakles victorious over Geryon, then Theseus becomes, structurally at least, the hero of the Amazonomachy—two sides of the
structure are devoted to Herakles, one to Theseus, one to the
Amazonomachy which is thus assimilated to the accomplishments
of the Athenian hero. The imbalance created in the organization
of the representations and the double participation in the
Themiskyra battle shift attention to Theseus.

The treasury at Delphi, as a mythical programmatic text,
began to effect the redistribution of legendary emphasis away from
the conquest of foreign lands, began to center discourse on the
local hero and his achievements. Herakles rooted out aboriginal
beasts and made new territory safe for settlement; Theseus
opened up Attica to the free movement of trade and established
Athenian hegemony over the land which it claimed by means of
the legend. The placement of the Amazonomachy on the treasury
appropriated the myth of the Amazons to the project of Athens.
It altered the significance of the Amazons, who were in the myth

of Herakles the inhabitants of land at the boundaries, at the far north-east of the world. The representation of the myth on the treasury left the mythical scheme open for its further development in the fifth century, when the later Amazon battle with Theseus, the battle in Attica, became the favorite episode to be illustrated.

The Delphic program shows its double, transitional nature formally as well as thematically. The metope structure of the treasury preserves the features of a duel, of the single hero poised in combat against a single bestial enemy. Like the patterned confrontations of the simpler vase paintings, and even more distinctly, the metope sets a frame around the *agôn* and centers the point of view.[35] There is no movement outside the frame; the instant of contact and resistance is frozen eternally in the form. On the east side of the Delphi treasury, each metope shows an Amazon or a Greek; on several, Amazons advance to the left without opponents. On the remaining four metopes, each Amazon is engaged in a duel with a Greek, with a victorious Amazon on one of the slabs. Von Bothmer identifies S1 as containing Theseus with an Amazon[36]—the work of art depicts the end of the fight, with the Amazon figure almost lifeless.

The Amazonomachy maintains the structure of a single hero beset by a monstrous opponent, paralleled on the other metopes which show the labors of the two heroes against beasts and criminals of the archaic world. Herakles defeats the Cretan bull just as he slays an Amazon (N9).[37] The metopes preserve the archaic duel structure, but they also point forward to a new conception of opposition, even of mirroring, between enemies. The series shows Theseus, hero of the *polis* rather than of the colony, combatting an army. He is confronted not simply by a single-, double-, or triple-bodied monster as enemy, but by an organized band, a group of Amazons ordered as an army. Troops arrive to support the falling queen, and the hero himself is aided by a band of companions, the warriors who accompany him. Hero^1: monster^1::Hero^2: monster^2.

The nature of heroism and therefore the idea of the norm have changed with the solidification of the *polis.* Here the change is represented on the level of the artistic text. As has often been remarked, the gradual change from the archaic *oikos* form of social organization to that of the city involved a change in military as well as familial organization.[38] In the traditional aristocratic, almost Homeric form of battle, the solitary warrior battled with the aid of his charioteer in single combat.[39] Enmity, and difference, were expressed through the positioning of man against man, man against beast. The confrontation between Glaukos and Diomedes, in *Iliad* 6, exemplifies this structure of enmity and difference because it is an exception to the rule of the *agôn*, the metope-like encounter of hero and hero. Because of forms of exchange, because of gift-giving in the past, the enmity of these heroes is erased; they are included in a world in which endogamy might occur, in which men are bound together through exchange. They cannot fight to death because they are implicated in a network of exchange patterns, in the dissolution of polarized opposition.

In contrast, the *polis* organized battle through the troop of hoplites, citizens who fought on foot in light armor, in large units. The organization of warfare recapitulated the democratic structure of the city as it had helped to create it. The matter of war became not simply the affair of a warrior, but rather the business of the whole *politeia*. The shift predates the elaborate work of art on the Athenian treasury at Delphi; the changing idea of battle is expressed in the forms of the sculpture. Theseus, though he fights in single combat with the Amazon queen, fights as the hero of the *polis*. As Herakles fights Geryon, the archaic triple monster, emblematic of the threatening armed figure who menaced the aristocratic hero of the past, so Theseus confronts the collectivity of women whose territory is Themiskyra. The work of art prepares the theme of the Amazonomachy for a new significance, a new use of the tradition to be worked out in the fifth century.

The concerns of the classical age, its focus on the hero, on an attempt to redefine heroism and the hero, to establish a norm for the warrior, involved a consideration of humanness, maleness, Greekness, in terms of opposition. The themes which were introduced on the Athenian treasury, a significant space on which to depict the myth since it celebrated, essentially without cult overtones, the wealth of Athena's city, were traced further in subsequent masterpieces of fifth-century sculpture. The myth of the Amazons became the property of the city of Athens, to be used again and again, up through the time of Isocrates. It was used in fifth-century art within a network of narrative structures to present a discourse on the differentiation of kinds. How are human beings different from animals? How are women different from men? How are Greeks different from barbarians? All these questions are posed in the context of the city, in the environment which the heroic Theseus was said to have founded, where men understood themselves to be bound together by sameness, by *isonomia*, by a common destiny and space, by endogamy. As J.-P. Vernant has shown, the hearth of the *oikos* became a common hearth, *hestia*, of the whole city, the center of a democratic circle in which equals were contained. Only when that center, that circumference, had been established could men begin to question what stood outside the boundary.[40]

The second monumental sculptural program to be discussed is the Parthenon, the building which summarized and celebrated Athens' pride and sense of herself in a moment of glory. But before I examine the role of the Amazonomachy and Centauromachy metopes played in the sculptural program of the temple of Athena, certain themes in the Centaur and Amazon myths and their representation must be recalled. Their placement in particular in the painted works of Mikon, now lost, has traditionally been associated with allegorical representations of the advance of the Persians into Greece, as mentioned above. These paintings apparently influenced much contemporary vase painting, and may have contributed to the vocabulary of sculptural forms as well.

The paintings in the Theseion are especially interesting, since the building was constructed by Cimon on the occasion of his returning of the bones of Theseus to Athens. Podlecki believes he was suggesting a connection between Miltiades and Theseus; the hero of the Persian wars was made analogous to the legendary victor over the Amazons and Centaurs. The ideas of cultural boundaries, of the role of Amazons and Centaurs outside marriage, outside exchange, outside culture, made them ideal representatives of the Persians, invaders from outside human, that is, Greek culture. The Amazons, once set in Themiskyra and made analogous with Geryon, are made to invade the territory of the Athenians and threaten to destroy it. The formal changes in the representation of the Centauromachy, for example, bear out the suggestion that such works of art as the Theseion paintings have a new ideological significance.

The Theseion paintings altered the terms of the confrontation between Theseus and his enemies, according to the reconstructions of the paintings by art historians.[41] Rather than showing the raid on Themiskyra, or the encounter of Herakles with the Centaurs on Mount Pholoe, they showed the invasion by the troop of Centaurs of the wedding of Peirithoös and the invasion of the Amazons to reclaim their queen from Athens. In addition to the change in the nature of the enemy represented, from a single opponent to a group, the altered environment of the Centauromachy shows, according to Susan Woodford, "a new ethical dimension."

> The traditional type [setting the Centauromachy in the open rather than at the wedding feast] often depicted the Centauromachy either as a simple conflict of man and monster or as a demonstration of the advantages of superior weaponry, but there was never any suggestion of moral overtones in such representations. The portrayal of the Centauromachy at the feast was new in art, and presented an ethical reinterpretation of the theme in terms of the struggle of civilization against barbarity.[42]

As she points out, the iconography surrounding Herakles had limitations, since it was concerned with a single individual.[43] The transformation of the theme rendered it applicable to the Persian Wars, where the Greeks fought as a group, not as individual heroes, against the barbarians. The new emphasis in art on the Amazons' invasion of Attica allowed the mythical material to serve in a similar way as an examination of the threat from *outside* Greek culture, of the difference which marked those within the city as human, civilized, cultured.

The Parthenon, one of the most beautiful and complex artifacts ever created by humankind, cannot be discussed fully here.[44] Most important in terms of this study is the relationship among the metopes, pediments and frieze, which reveals emphasis on the themes of civilization and barbarity, as does the important Centauromachy pediment at Olympia.[45] There is an interesting temporal dimension to the various aspects of the Parthenon's sculptural program. In addition to a Gigantomachy and a representation of the sack of Troy, the Parthenon metopes bore a Centauromachy and an Amazonomachy, which paralleled each other on east and west sides of the building. Thus in the archaic metope form, the agonistic, time-freezing qualities of the duel, the single combat, were preserved, while the frieze rendered the perpetual motion and continuity of the contemporary city, its citizens, its rituals, even its gods. The pediments display moments of origin—the birth of Athena, the moment in which she became patron of the city. Thus there is a temporal progression from absolute origin, on the pediments, to the fixity of archaic time on the metopes, to the flux of the eternal present, represented in the frieze. The reality of the *polis*, its repeated performance of the ceremonies of the Panathenaia, were made continuous with the reality of its first audience, just as the ceremony at the end of the *Oresteia* enters the world of its audience and claims them as participants.[46] The metopes, showing Centaurs and Amazons, the part of the program which concerns us most, placed the enemies of civilization and of the city outside, poised at the boundaries, in opposition but without the power of movement.[47] The static form of the duels marks the Amazons and Centaurs—as other, as excluded absolutely both from the origins and from the present reality of Athens.

The metopes which depict the Amazonomachy are barely distinguishable, while many of the Centaur/Lapith duels are beautifully preserved. In these metopes, now in the British Museum, the bodies of the Centaurs consist of clearly human torsoes set onto the forelegs and backs of horses. The Centaurs are more than half human, more than half horse; their facial expressions are depicted with great sensitivity. They are less bestial than the Centaurs of the earlier period, yet their determination to conquer is distilled and intensified in the humanness of their faces. While the Amazon metopes are mutilated, there is another object which may be reconstructed and on which the Amazonomachy was represented—the famous shield of Athena Parthenos which once belonged, with the monumental statue, inside the Parthenon.[48] The Strangford shield shows in part the structure of this representation in the round—according to Pausanias, the sculptor Pheidias portrayed both himself and Pericles as participants in the battle. Their presence emphasizes the analogy made between the legendary invasion of the Amazons, the invasion of the Persians, and the supposed enemies of the mid-fifth century *polis*, those who would disrupt the circle of citizenship and violate the boundaries drawn by the Athenians.[49] Pericles' law of 451, redefining endogamy by limiting citizenship to those both of whose parents were citizens, can be seen in this light as an attempt to establish boundaries, to distinguish strictly among kinds and to define the norm by exclusion. The whole of the Parthenon can be seen as a similar project, as a structure which celebrates Athens, focuses on its unity, and closes a circle. The Amazons and Centaurs represented on the metopes are emblematic of all that the city closes out. Their bestial, single-sex cultures, their chaotic, disordered, unruly force, must be set in contrast to the ordered, reverent progress of the Athenians. The mythical beings are seen both as violent and as fixed forever outside, poised in opposition to the Greek warriors at the boundaries of the *polis*.

On the last of the monuments to be discussed, the Centauromachy and the Amazonomachy are juxtaposed in a continuous frieze. The temple of Apollo Epikourios at Bassae falls outside the geographical boundaries of Attica, but if Rhys Carpenter is correct in following the ancient tradition, its architect was Iktinos, the architect of the Parthenon, and it thus can be interpreted in light of its relationship to the Parthenon program.[50] The temple has recently been exhaustively studied by Charline Hofkes-Brukker and Alfred Mallwitz, in an impressive work, *Der Bassai-Fries in der ursprünglich geplanten Anordnung*, which considers all the evidence concerning such problems as the placement of the frieze.[51] The temple presents many puzzles; for example, it is the only temple of the period known to have a frieze which encircles the inner room, the cella. It has other peculiarities, noted by Hofkes-Brukker, which are less relevant than this internal focus, and the continuous aspect of the frieze.

The frieze represents a break from the static duel form of metopes to a continuous discourse which links Centaurs and Amazons in a flow without a clear break. The Bassae frieze is punctuated by a slab showing Artemis and Apollo arriving at the Centauromachy to aid the Lapiths. They drive their chariot, pulled by two deer—thus the animal, the half-horse of the Centaurs, running wild in the Centauromachy, is set back into its proper relationship, harnessed and serving the gods. The Centauromachy shows the horse/men attacking female and male Lapiths sexually. They are horses with the heads and torsoes of old men, and like satyrs they assault humankind. On one slab, a Lapith woman takes refuge at the shrine of the goddess, and there is a significant "citation," an allusion to an older form of art, the static cult figure of archaic statuary which is thus included and superseded in this work.[52]

In the sequence of the frieze devoted to the Amazonomachy, the motifs resemble those of the extended battles of vase painting, with several Amazons and Greeks focused around a confrontation. Most interesting in the sequence is the slab showing Herakles, with his lion's skin draped around him, battling against what may be the Amazon's queen. It has been suggested that another panel shows Theseus, also at Themiskyra, although the evidence for this identification is not definitive.[53] The Herakles panel (541) depicts a mounted Amazon moving from left to right, over a fallen Greek, an Amazon facing Herakles, who is shown with his body facing front, his head turned toward her, and on the right a strangely twisted group which recalls the Amazon/Geryon analogy made earlier. Here the Amazon is contorted over the back of a horse, so that she resembles the figure of a Centaur, while a Greek, from behind and above, is forcing her and seems to form part of a tripartite being.

In this elaborate graphic "text" the analogy between Amazons and Centaurs is made explicitly, since the discourse is unbroken. On metopes, attention is focused on individual encounters, on the difference between the bodies of Lapiths and Centaurs, on the hybrid bestiality of the horse/men, poised in eternal contrast to the beautiful, youthful forms of the Lapiths. Here a more explicit equation is made between the exclusively male culture of the Centaurs, sexually aggressive and violent, and the exclusively female culture of the Amazons, equally violent yet beautiful.

The form of the representations emphasizes a change in the ideas of difference which are the implicit theme of these works of art. The enemy—the other—is no longer simply a marker at the boundary by which the culture defines itself in opposition, as in the program of the Parthenon. The enemy has entered the temple itself and is displayed within, in combat with men. Perhaps this fact explains the peculiar interior structure of the temple, which had a distinctly separate second inner room, the *adyton*, which Carpenter believes may have contained the cult statue.[54] In this case, the presence of these enemies of civilization, the horse/men, the horse-women of myth, might have been seen as trespassers in the sacred space devoted to the god.[55] Their invasion of the temple space necessitated another, more sacred spot in which the god rested alone. The unusual setting of the frieze may have had other causes, since the temple was situated on a particularly lonely height in Arcadia, distant from the *polis* which constructed it.[56] The frieze's internal placement however effects an enclosure of the temple on itself, fencing out hostile nature and focusing attention on the human space within, which is thus differentiated from the unworked stone of the hillside. Unlike other temples, the Apollo temple was not built simply to fit into a landscape, to form a whole with the rest of the mountain; its construction emphasized the exclusive quality of temple space and thus altered the relationship between inside and out which was typical of Greek sacred architecture.[57]

These three monuments—the Athenian treasury at Delphi, the Parthenon, the Apollo temple—reveal a change in speculation about difference, from the period of the late sixth century to the twenties of the fifth century, when the sculpture of the Bassae temple was probably set in place. The metopes of the Athenian treasury at Delphi effect a transformation of mythical material about fantastic beings, the Amazons, appropriating them into the mythology of Athens, making an explicit analogy through juxtaposition between the labors of Herakles and those of Theseus. The metope form stresses the static qualities of the confrontations between Herakles and his traditional enemies, who are polarized in opposition to one another. Theseus becomes Herakles' replacement in the thinking of the democratic polis, as a hero who encounters the other—the Amazons—and by defeating them establishes boundaries at the edge of the world within which the *polis* will define itself. The builders of the Parthenon, along with those who created the monumental paintings of the mid-fifth

century, used the analogy between Centaurs, Amazons, and barbarians, to represent the victory of the *polis* over the Persians, and
to celebrate the city in its *isonomia*, its homogeneity. The citizens
are shown not as mythical beings but as ritual celebrants, while
the enemies of their ritual, their culture, are set on the boundaries
of the temple, on the metopes as on the limits of culture. The
human combatants on the metopes preserve the sacred space,
fixed in static opposition to the forces of animality, chaos, and
sexual violence which Centaurs and Amazons exemplify. On the
Bassae frieze, the elements of violence have entered that sacred
space, and the analogy between the two kinds of hybrid beings is
made explicit. They are linked in their violence in an attack
which is made circular, through the enclosing form of the frieze,
one which is endless and has invaded culture. The aggression and
monstrosity of these traditional enemies of civilization have
become part of the city's most sacred space, and they operate continuously from inside. The chaotic forces of bestiality, of sexuality, of barbarism, are reinterpreted. They no longer stand at the
limits of culture. They have been acknowledged as elements to be
combatted within. The presence of Apollo and Artemis within the
work of art is an appeal for transcendence, for a divine force or an
internal power which will preserve the demarcations between male
and female, human and animal, Greek and barbarian.

Examination of these works of art reveals a progression, a
change in ideas about difference which will be taken up further in
later chapters. For the moment I would like to discuss further the
elements these works of art have in common, the ways in which
they use mythic material to center on what is defined as the norm,
the subject of culture.

Through the Amazonomachies and Centauromachies, the
barbarians were defined through analogy as paradoxically bestial,
controlled by appetite rather than by reason, enslaved like the
Centaurs to desire, and as females garbed in armor, a grotesque,
often seductive parody of an army. Within the artistic text, the
two myths define the victorious Greeks, in polar opposition to
these two alternative, asymmetrical versions of barbarian culture.
Persians, barbarians, cannot participate in the civilizing relationships of exchange and marriage because they are mythically analogous to the Centaurs, violent and exclusively male, as well as

half-animal. They are mythically equivalent to the Amazons as well, invaders from the East who are exclusively female and who resist with violence the giving of women in marriage. Barbarians are anti-culture, incapable of engaging in exchange, defined through analogy as outside the bounds of culture, to be warred against and excluded.

Through the reciprocity of analogy, the works of art define alien, monstrous, female. Animals are clearly outside human culture; the Centaurs' bestiality makes them violent and greedy, and their animality is the more repulsive since they share human desires as well. The myth of the Amazons, in contrast, serves to define and differentiate female from male by isolating femaleness. The analogy among barbarians, animals, and females brings into particular prominence the difference between male and female. Barbarians and animals are clearly "other"; females are clearly defined as such through analogy with them. The contradictions of the marriage/culture metaphor are thus revealed with great intensity. Men exchange women, therefore men make culture, yet they cannot do so without women, who are by this definition of culture-as-exchange excluded from civilization. Women are both inside and outside culture. The myth of the Amazons is a particularly valuable key to understanding the representation of women in the theory of the Greeks, and more will be said about it in the subsequent chapter on male/female difference.

The representations of Amazons and Centaurs in the works of art of the sixth and fifth centuries show that myths were used to elaborate and sustain ideas of racial, sexual, and species difference. In the classical period, the juxtaposition and subsequent analogy served to supply a definition of *man*—the Greek male—as the sole significant figure of culture. It is he, not-female, not-animal, not-barbarian, who is the subject of endogamous marriage and thus of culture itself.

There is a supporting historical proposition laid out in the juxtaposition in graphic art of the Centauromachy and Amazonomachy. The existence of the Centaurs can be accounted for through a phylogenetic theory, that of the Amazons by a theory of ontogeny. If their mythical origins are forgotten, the Centaurs represent a species belonging to a stage prior to human evolution. They are not the product of human intercourse with a horse, as their bodily forms suggest, but rather a vestigial race, anachronistically present at a historical stage which had superseded them. According to Aetius, Empedocles had formulated an evolutionary theory of human history which would account for the Centaurs:

> Empedocles held that the first generations of animals and plants were not complete but consisted of separate limbs not joined together; the second, arising from the joining of these limbs, were like creatures in dreams [*eidôlophaneis*]; the third was the generation of whole-natured forms; and the fourth arose no longer from the homoeomerous substances such as earth and water, but by generation, in some cases as the result of the condensation of their nourishment, in others because feminine beauty [*eumorphias*] excited the sexual urge; and the various species of animals were distinguished [*diakrithênai*] by the quality of the mixture in them. . . .[58]

According to Empedocles, the Centaurs—part horse, part man— were a remnant of prehistory, a species from the time before species differentiation.

The Amazons, on the other hand, represent a stage in the evolution of the individual human being before sexual differentiation. There were many cross-sexual rituals of puberty and initiation among the Greeks, and such myths as that of Achilles and his transvestite youth touch on this theme.[59] As Vernant argues, the ritual exchange of dress in initiation ceremonies was a temporary participation in the other sex which preceded the distinct separation of the sexes in adulthood.[60] The Hubristica of Argos was one such ceremony in which young women dressed as men and engaged in combat. Herodotos in his description of the Auses, a Libyan tribe, told of a festival of Athena which involved ritual combat on the part of young girls (4.180 ff.). Thus the Amazons represent a preadolescent female/ male being, where the transvestism and male attributes of the women complement their worship of the huntress Artemis and the war god Ares. This reading of the myth and of its representation in the artistic texts leads, like the encounter with the Centaurs, to the Greek male youth, the victor in both Amazonomachy and Centauromachy. He is represented as the *telos*, the proper end of both phylogenetic and ontogenetic evolution. The juxtaposition of the Amazonomachy and Centauromachy offers a brief, doubled prehistory of the city. There is as well an allegory about the Greek victory over the barbarians, and a proposition about marriage, about the necessity for a closed endogamous system of exchange of women.

Another proposition is being tested in works of art like the Bassae frieze, where the analogy between Amazons and Centaurs is made explicit. There is an attempt to situate man between animal and female, to make real a fantasy of masculine *autarkeia*, self-sufficiency.

ANIMAL----Centaur----HUMAN MALE----Amazon----FEMALE
        (animal/male)   (male/female)

On a horizontal axis, if one extreme is animal, then the Centaurs represent a mid-point between animals and men. At the other extreme are women, with Amazons occupying a mediating position. They are female, yet have male attributes of warlikeness and aggression. There is no hierarchy of difference; men are a perfect balance between these analogous alternatives, a marriage, self-contained, between animal and female nature. The fantasy recalls the myth told by Hesiod of the time when gods and men lived in community, when there were no women, when men did not have to hunt or labor in the fields. Man was self-sufficient then and his nostalgia for self-sufficiency, for wholeness, is re-enacted in the works of art.[61] There man is self-contained, and his state depicts a return to the past, to a time before marriage, before work, and before women.[62]

The representation of the Centauromachy/Amazonomachy in works of sculptural art confirms and extends the propositions generated from an analysis of the two bodies of myth about the horse/men, horse-women. The myths centered around themes of culture and hostility to culture; the earlier forms of the myths treated gift-exchange and the violation of that institution. Later, marriage became the metaphor through which ideas of culture, and the boundaries of culture, were expressed. Both Amazons and Centaurs were outside the limits of humanness. By extension, on works of art especially after the defeat of the Persian invasion early in the fifth century, the mythical opponents of humans—Centaurs and Amazons—were ideal representations of the barbarian invaders. Through the analogy among barbarians, Centaurs, and Amazons, all served in speculation about difference to define the cultural norm, the human Greek male who was set in opposition to the strange, half-human creatures.

Centaurs and Amazons, and by extension animals and females, were linked with barbarians analogously, as the "other" through which the subject of *polis* culture, the male citizen, came to know himself. The forces outside the city—violence and disorder, forms of community which were asymmetrical sexually, which had no way of reproducing themselves, which were deformed alternatives to the democratic institutions—were thus seen as equivalent and threatening. The citizen and his city celebrated themselves in resistance to these threats by exposing the others' chaotic bestial qualities, their invasive, disruptive intentions, by setting them in static, frozen forms at the boundaries of the living process of the city's ritual, as on the Parthenon.

In the process of defining the city by defining its limits, other propositions about the nature of civilization were elaborated as well. The metaphor of marriage as culture was expressed contradictorily, since it placed women both outside the city, as Amazons bent on invasion and on the destruction of marriage, and as brides, the objects of exchange, the necessary means by which the city was to reproduce itself. The theme of masculine *autarkeia*, a persistent notion in Greek thinking, was a solution on the level of speculation and myth-making to this problematic. Man was not only different from animal, woman, barbarian; his culture could stand alone, in harmony with the gods as in the past.

In the chapters which follow, the analogical network of difference will be examined in greater detail, in particular as it was expressed in tragedy, a crucial ritual and political occasion of fifth century life. The mode of reasoning through polarity and analogy will be seen to have general applicability throughout the century, but also to reach its limits with the second great war of the *polis*.

NOTES

1.   Erwin Panofsky, "Iconography and Iconology: An Introduction to the Study of Renaissance Art," in *Meaning in the Visual Arts* (Harmondsworth, 1970), pp. 51 ff.

2.   Ibid., p. 66. "Iconology, then, is a method of interpretation which arises from synthesis rather than analysis" [58]. In this sense, Panofsky's project corresponds to that of the followers of Lovejoy.

3.   See von Bothmer, op. cit., *passim*, Baur, op. cit., *passim*, Barron, op. cit.; Shefton, op. cit.; C. Robert, *Kentaurenkampf und Tragödienscene* (Halle, 1898); P. Oelschig, *De Centauromachiae in arte graeca figuris* (Halle, 1911); Charles H. Morgan, "The Sculptures of the Hephaisteion I, II," *Hesp.* 31 (1962): 210-35, especially Appendix III, "The Decline of the Repugnant," 233; E.B. Harrison, "The Composition of the Amazonomachy on the Shield of Athena Parthenos," *Hesp.* 35 (1966): 109-33; and on Centauromachies, P.E. Corbett, *Gnomon* 43 (1971): 65 ff.

4.   See, for example, Gisela M.A. Richter, *The Sculpture and Sculptors of the Greeks* (New Haven, 1970, 4th rev. ed.). Notable exceptions are Vincent Scully's *The Earth, The Temple, and the Gods. Greek Sacred Architecture* (New Haven and London, 1962) which attempts to situate Greek art as a historical and cultural phenomenon, and the work of J.J. Pollitt, *Art and Experience in Classical Greece* (Cambridge, 1972); and more recently Herbert Hoffman, *Sexual and Asexual Pursuit: A Structuralist Approach to Greek Vase Painting* (London, 1977).

5.   von Bothmer, op. cit., pl. 33, 1.

6.   Ibid., p. 40.

7.   I mean by "opposition" here only that one side of the vase bears one image, the opposite side another.

8.   On sculpture, coins, and literature, see Marc Shell, *The Economy of Literature* (Baltimore and London, 1978), especially pp. 63 ff.: "The Language of Character: An Introduction to a Poetics of Monetary Inscriptions."

9.   See G.M.A. Richter, *Attic Red-Figured Vases, A Survey*, rev. ed. (New Haven, 1958), pp. 141 ff.

10.   See John Boardman, *Pre-Classical. From Crete to Archaic Greece* (Harmondsworth, 1967), and W. Schadewelt, *Von Homers Welt und Werk*, 2nd ed. (Stuttgart, 1951), pp. 130-54.

11.   "Hestia-Hermès. Sur l'expression religieuse de l'espace et du mouvement chez les Grecs," in *Mythe et pensée*, vol. I, 101 ff.

12. . . . le couple Hermès-Hestia exprime, dans sa polarité, la tension qui se marque dans la représentation archaïque de l'espace: l'espace exige un centre, un point fixe, à valeur privilégiée, à partir duquel on puisse orienter et définir des directions, toutes différentes qualitativement; mais l'espace se presente en même temps comme lieu du mouvement, ce qui implique une possibilité de transition et de passage de n'importe quel passage à un autre.

Ibid., p. 101.

13. Ibid., p. 1. On Hermes paired with Apollo, at one of the six altars at Olympia, see Herodorus *FGH* 1.31.34, *ap. Schol. in Pind.* 01. 5.5/10a.

14. Lloyd, op. cit., p. 6. His position differs from Lévi-Strauss'; see *The Savage Mind* (Chicago, 1966) in which the latter argues for the "kaleidoscopic" logic of so-called primitive societies, p. 36.

15. Kirk, op. cit., p. 171.

16. For critiques of the Lévi-Straussian analysis, see Anthony Wilden, *System and Structure: Essays in Communication and Exchange* (London, 1972); John Peradotto, "Oedipus and Erichthonius: Some Observations on Paradigmatic and Syntagmatic Order," *Arethusa* 10, 1 (Spring 1977): 85 ff.; and in the same volume, J.S. Turner, "Narrative Structure and Mythopoesis: A Critique and Reformulation of Structuralist Concepts of Myth, Narrative, and Poetics," 103-62.

17. For a classicist's critique of this essay, see Perradotto, ibid.

18. Snell, op. cit., p. 35. M. Detienne points out to me that the Persians were also associated with the giants, and thus both with chaos.

19. von Bothmer, op. cit., p. 6.

20. Bernard Ashmole, *Architect and Sculptor in Classical Greece* (London, 1972), pp. 165 ff.

21. Thus, among others Brian Cook, a curator of the Bassae frieze at the British Museum, in his introduction to the collection, *The Frieze of the Temple of Apollo at Bassae* (London, no date), p. 8.

22. Sobol, op. cit., p. 90.

23. Roger Hinks, *Myth and Allegory in Ancient Art* (London, 1939), p. 65.

24. Ibid., p. 13.

25. Ibid., p. 65.

26. Snell, op. cit., p. 35.

27.   Anthony J. Podlecki, *The Political Background of Aeschylean Tragedy* (Ann Arbor, 1966), pp. 8 ff.

28.   *Fouilles de Delphes*, 15 vols., 18 fascicules, 1902 ff.

29.   William Bell Dinsmoor, *The Architecture of Ancient Greece, An Account of its Historic Development*, 3rd rev. ed., (London, 1950), p. 117, and *AJA* 50 (1946): 86 ff.; von Bothmer, op. cit., pp. 118 ff.

30.   See Plutarch, *Life of Theseus.*

31.   G. Karl Galinsky, *The Herakles Theme. The Adaptations of the Hero in Literature from Homer to the Twentieth Century* (Oxford, 1972), p. 41.

32.   M. Bowra, *Greek Lyric Poetry*, 2nd ed. (Oxford, 1961), p. 89.

33.   But see Susan Woodford, *Exemplum Virtutis: A Study of Heracles in Athens in the Second Half of the Fifth Century B.C.* (Columbia University Dissertation: 1966).

34.   Martin P. Nilsson, *Cults, Myths, Oracles and Politics in Ancient Greece* (Lund, 1951), p. 55.

35.   On the agonistic style of Greek culture, see Alvin Gouldner, *The Hellenic World, A Sociological Analysis* (Part I of *Enter Plato*) (New York, 1969), pp. 41-74.

36.   von Bothmer, op. cit.

37.   Fritz Saxl, in "Continuity and Variation in the Meaning of Images," traces the occurrence of man battling bull from Syrian and Akkadian art, through representations of Herakles and Nessos, Herakles and the stag, a Lapith fighting a Centaur, to the late Amazon sarcophagus now at Hampton Court; ". . . even the fight with the Amazons shows clear traces of our image: the conqueror is kneeling on the Amazon in exactly the same way as Hercules kneels on the animal in Delphi and Olympia." The image is revived in the representations of Mithras as bull-killer, and of Samson, the Hercules of the Bible, defeating the lion (12th century A.D.). *Lectures*, 2 vols. (London, 1957), pp. 1-12.

38.   J.-P. Vernant, ed., *Problèmes de la guerre en Grèce ancienne* (Paris and The Hague, 1968). See also P. Vidal-Naquet, "La tradition de l'hoplite athénien," in *Le chasseur noir. Formes de pensée et formes de société dans le monde grec* (Paris, 1981), pp. 125-149.

39.   See Francis Vian, "La fonction guerrière dans la mythologie grecque," in Vernant, *Problèmes . . .* , pp. 53-68.

40.   Vernant, *Mythe et pensée*, p. 158.

41.   Barron, op. cit., discusses other opinions on the Theseion.

42.   Susan Woodford, "More Light on Old Walls: The Theseus of the Centauromachy in the Theseion," *JHS* 94 (1974): 161.

43. Ibid., p. 162. Woodford also mentions the importance of rape as a theme in art in the years after the Persian wars. On feasting as a political act, see Florence Dupont, *Le Plaisir et la loi* (Paris, 1977), pp. 19-26.

44. See, among others, Martin Robertson, *The Parthenon Frieze* (London, 1975), with bibliography; Scully, op. cit., pp. 171-85; Rhys Carpenter, *The Architects of the Parthenon* (Harmondsworth, 1970); von Bothmer, op. cit., p. 208.

45. Hinks, op. cit., p. 28.

46. Robertson calls it "the ideal embodiment of a recurrent festival," op. cit., p. 11. On the Panathenaia, see H.W. Parke, *Festivals of the Athenians* (London, 1977), pp. 33-50.

47. Scully, on the other hand, says of the metopes:

> . . . the bodies of Centaur and Lapith, and probably those of the other archetypal antagonists, merge into single organisms: men and animals, Greek and Amazon, gods and giants, the upper and nether modes of life, the slayer and the slain. All at last is one.

Op. cit., p. 183. The iconography of these scenes, however, suggests quite the opposite; the Centaurs and Amazons, as figures for the barbarians, are rather shown in their radical otherness from their opponents. Compare the Centaurs on the Olympia pediment.

48. E.B. Harrison, "The Composition of the Amazonomachy on the Shield of Athena Parthenos," *Hesp.* 35 (1966): 109-33.

49. Yvon Garlan's remarks on Pericles' military strategy are interesting in this regard. Pericles sacrificed defence of the countryside to the defence of the city, in contrast to the traditional strategy.

> Le projet stratégique realisé par Périclès était, eu égard à la territoire terrestre de Sparte, la condition nécessaire du développement de l'impérialisme. . . . C'était une arme que se donnaient les Athéniens, non sans sacrifice . . . pour parvenir au stade suprême d'expansion auquel pouvait prétendre une cité grecque.

"La défense du territoire à l'époque classique," in *Problèmes de la terre en Grèce ancienne*, M.I. Finley, ed., (Paris and The Hague, 1973), p. 159.

50. Carpenter, op. cit., pp. 142 ff. See also H. Knell, "Iktinos: Baumeister des Parthenon und des Asklepiostempels von Phigalia-Bassae," *Jahrbuch des deutschen archäologischen Instituts* 83 (1968): 100-17.

51.   Charline Hofkes-Brukker: *Der Bassai-Fries in der ursprünglich geplanten Anordnung.* Alfred Mallwitz, *Zur Architektur des Apollon-Tempels in Bassai-Phigalia* (Munich, 1975), especially pp. 45-119, on iconography and the composition of the frieze. Earlier works include Dinsmoor, op. cit., 154-59; H. Kenner, *Der Fries des Tempels von Bassae-Phigalia* (Vienna, 1946); C.R. Cockerell, *The Temples of Jupiter Panhellenius at Aegina and of Apollo Epicurius near Phigaleia in Arcadia* (1860).

52.   Hofkes-Brukker notes the unusual iconography of the Centauromachy, which depicts neither the battle outdoors nor the marriage feast, but rather a raid on this Artemis' sanctuary.

53.   Ibid, op. cit. See also von Bothmer, op. cit., pp. 215-16, for a summary of the debate.

54.   Carpenter, op. cit., p. 150. See also F.A. Cooper, "The Temple of Apollo at Bassae: New Observations on its Plan and Orientation," *AJA* 72 (1968): 103-11.

55.   Scully says of the frieze that its figures

> . . . are like the surrounding mountains brought inside, awkward and thunderous, and they engage in the contest which is one part of the meaning of the temple as a whole: man against the beast power in nature, man against the old ways.

Op. cit., p. 126. See also Robert L. Scranton, *Aesthetic Aspects of Ancient Art* (Chicago and London, 1964), p. 191.

56.   Scully, op. cit., pp. 123-4.

57.   Scully, ibid., p. 46. For another view, see C.A. Doxiadis, *Architectural Space in Ancient Greece*, trans. and ed. by Jaqueline Tyrwhitt (Cambridge, Mass. and London, 1972); and Christian Norberg-Schulz, *Meaning in Western Architecture* (New York, 1975), pp. 44-80.

58.   Kirk and Raven, op. cit., #442, p. 336: Aetius 5.19.5, (DK 31A 72). Aelian cites another Heraclitean fragment, 61, in *Nat. anim.*:

> Many creatures were born with faces and breasts on both sides, man-faced ox-progeny, while others again sprang forth as ox-headed offspring of man, creatures compounded partly of male, partly of the nature of female, and fitted with shadowy (or sterile, Diels) parts.
>
> [16.29]

Kirk and Raven, #446, p. 337. See also Bollack and Wismann, op. cit.

59.   During the Oschophoria, a festival celebrated during Pyanepsion, two well-born young men wearing female robes

headed the procession from Athens to Phaleron, supposedly in memory of a trick Theseus played in Minos, when he dressed two youths as girls. See Parke, op. cit., pp. 77-79.

60. ... pour chaque sexe, l'initiation qui l'accomplit dans sa qualité spécifique d'homme ou de femme peut comporter, par l'échange rituel de vêtements, la participation momentanée à la nature de l'autre sexe dont il va devenir en se séparant de lui, le complément.

"La guerre des cités," *Mythe et société*, p. 39.

61. See Pucci, op. cit.

62. Note Lévi-Strauss' similar longing for a golden age, in his *Tristes Tropiques*, trans. by J. and D. Weightman (New York, 1974), p. 313; and P. duBois, "Tristes Topiques": Framing the Woman Question," *Mass. Review* 21:2 (Summer 1980): 334-42.

III

Greeks And Barbarians

It is commonplace, in discussion of the idea of racial difference in Western culture, to point out that the ancient world had no racial prejudice, that the Greeks and Romans were not subject to the racial hatred which has characterized later centuries, especially since the period of Western colonization in the fifteenth and sixteenth centuries A.D.[1] In fact, the Greeks seem not to have considered color as an overriding mark of racial difference, but not for the motives of humanism or democracy suggested by some latter-day critics. Perhaps one of the reasons skin color was not an important sign of racial difference was, as will be discussed later in considering male/female difference, that color opposition, in works of art at least, was reserved for difference between the sexes.[2]

Yet difference between Greeks and barbarians was a strongly marked, deeply felt opposition in the thinking of the Greeks. Barbarians were "other," and the Greeks were at some periods much concerned with their difference; the interest of the Hellenes in alien cultures, especially in the years of colonization, was proverbial. Much of Herodotos' fascinating text on the Persian Wars treats the ideas of physical and cultural difference throughout the Mediterranean world.[3]

If it is true that the Greeks, unlike their heirs, did not inflict color prejudice on others, it was because another, in their eyes more significant, factor effaced difference of skin color, and that was the difference of language. They distinguished between *Hellenes*, Greek speakers, and *barbaroi*, babblers.[4] This marker of the difference between Greeks and barbarians emerged when a shared language of discourse became a crucial political fact. In Homer, barbarians, or those who would later be considered barbarians, and "Danaoi" spoke a common hybrid language, the language of the oral formulaic style, which embodied elements of several dialects as well as features from a period long before the composition of the poem.[5] There was no attempt to distinguish the language of the Trojans from that of the Danaans; the marking of difference through language, as for example in the portrait of the Phrygian slave of Euripides' *Orestes*, did not occur to the singer of the Homeric songs.

Only with the development of the *polis*, its politics through discussion in the assembly, the use of language as well as hereditary power to influence the community, did the distinction between barbarian and Greek become a crucially important defining opposition. The Greek defeat of the Persians in the Persian Wars, which ended in 478, added support to the Greeks' ideas of differentiation through language. Those wars were won in part because of the solidarity of democratic Athens, its development in the previous century from a village surrounded by outlying farms into a *polis* with a centralized system of governing, an assembly. Discussion took place in the *agora*, in a common language which bound the city together with other cities like it, whose citizens met at the games, at the oracles.[6] And within those cities, the citizens engaged in increasingly restricted marital exchanges.

The practice of endogamy bound together the citizens of the *polis*, as did their common language, in opposition to those excluded from relations of verbal and marital exchange. J.-P. Vernant has shown that the Greeks conceived of marriage as complemented by another institution, war; they opposed *philia* to *polemos*, powers complementary in their opposition.[7] Those who spoke the same language exchanged women; those outside, *barbaroi*, could not be included in marital exchange and were thus enemies in war as well. The polarizing tendency of early Greek philosophical discourse is well exemplified in the doublet Greek/barbarian.

Herodotos bears testimony to the Greeks' ideas about barbarians when he recounts the reply of the Spartans to Xerxes' offer of power over lands in Greece, if only they would submit to him:

"Your counsels to us, Hydarnes, are ill assorted; one half of them rests on knowledge, but the other on ignorance; you know well how to be a slave, but you have never tasted of freedom, to know whether it be sweet or not [*eleutheriês de oukô epeirêthês, out'ei gluku out'ei mê*]. Were you to taste of it, not with spears you would counsel us to fight for it, no, but with axes."

[6.135]

The polarity of freedom/slavery is strengthened by the analogy with sweetness, one of the terms employed in philosophical and medical texts to delimit, through doublets, the realm of tastes.[8] In the same way that food was differentiated and defined through opposition, so the realm of politics was divided into Greek and barbarian, slavery and freedom. Spartans shared with other Greeks their use of the Greek language; barbarians, on the other side of the polarizing doublet, were characterized by slavishness, by their unwillingness to fight as free men did for freedom. The Persian troops fought under the lash, while the free Greeks went into battle to defend civilization.

The polarizing vision, dividing the universe of discourse into doublets which exclude each other, is reminiscent of the agonistic structure of the early classical metopes discussed in the previous chapter. There is a static quality in the individual metopes on the Athenian treasury at Delphi; each single unit is based on a confrontation between opposites. Each metope is composed in a frame, balanced inward, toward the moment of battle between enemies. Yet the whole tells a narrative of a larger confrontation between two nations, tells how each separate incident of meeting builds into a greater pattern of victory for the Greeks, defeat and capture for the Amazons.

Aeschylus' tragedy the *Persae* is structured on the same principles as the metopes of the temples of the early fifth century. It has a static quality often remarked by critics, who object to its almost motionless presentation of the Persian Court, of the sufferings of Atossa and Xerxes.[9] The only episodes of movement and energy are those in which the messenger describes the battle of Salamis, the scene in which the two great opponents are pitted against one another in an extended *agôn*. Atossa tells her tale, Darius speaks at length of his views on theology, *hubris*, and the follies of his son, Xerxes himself appears only to lament. There is little interaction among the various characters of the drama.

Yet there is a constant opposition being expressed throughout the performance of the *Persae*. The Greeks, who are never mentioned, who are almost compulsively excluded from representation, are the other side of the relationship of opposition. They appear only through negation, through the Persians' exposition of their own defeat. The Greeks provide the missing balance-weight, the other side of the opposition which gives the drama its significance. Thus the pattern of composition of the treasury metopes is echoed in the composition of the tragedy; a seemingly static series of units based on internal stress, when seen as a whole, reveals a larger pattern of opposition which provides a definition of two opponents, two kinds of beings. In the tragedy, only one side of the opposition is given. The agonistic relationship, the missing opponent, is to be supplied by the audience, which is thus required to define itself as the absent opposite of what is represented before them.

It is war, *polemos*, opposed to *philia*, love, which revealed the stress, the division between kinds of beings. Heraclitus says of war:

> War is the father of all and king of all, and some he shows as gods, others as men; some he makes slaves, other free [*polemos pantôn men patêr esti, pantôn de basileus, kai tous men theous edeixe tous de anthrôpous, tous men doulous epoiêse tous de eleutherous*].[10]

Heraclitus uses the concept war, *polemos*, to express metaphorically the principle of change which governs the cosmos, which divides kinds of things, which clarifies the difference between gods and men, slaves and free. In a more literal sense, *polemos*, the real fact of war, creates slaves, prisoners of war, victors. War reveals the nature of beings. The war between the Titans and the gods showed men to differ from the gods; the war between Greeks and Persians served to differentiate slave from free in an analogous manner. The showing forth of difference occurs in the situation of the *agôn*, the contest, the battle, just as likeness is manifested in the sharing of women, in the institution of marriage among Greeks. As the metope represented the *agôn* between man and beast, so the tragic drama, in its agonistic form, showed forth difference between the Greeks and their polar opposites, the foreign Persians. The Centauromachy and the Amazonomachy, in their analogous relationship to the Persian War, spoke of the institutions of war and marriage, institutions which marked the boundaries of the city. The *Persae*, which takes place entirely "outside," ends by showing the boundaries of the Hellenes, the circle within which culture exists.

The *Persae* is exceptional in the extant corpus of Greek tragedy.[11] It is perhaps the earliest of Aeschylus' works and was performed in 472 at the City Dionysia. It treats a subject from recent history, the aftermath of the battle of Salamis, which occurred in 480. No other tragic text which we possess so directly addressed a real event and had so clear a basis in history rather than myth, although in 493 Phrynichus presented a tragedy now lost which represented the fall of Miletus in 494 and which was banned by the Athenians.[12] The *Persae* violates the injunction against showing the present directly in the tragic amphitheater. Aeschylus' tragedy is played out entirely in Susa, the residence of the Persian kings; no Greek character speaks throughout the play. Thus the representation of the historic event occurs through inversion and distancing, through the device of Persian reaction to the events of Salamis.

This tragedy is not the only Aeschylean text to address the issue of barbarian difference, Persian or otherwise, as Helen Bacon points out.[13] In the *Suppliants*, for example, the issues of barbarity and endogamy are explicitly thematized.[14] Yet the *Persae*, because of its peculiarities, offers an especially rich example of the way in which the earliest of the tragedians reasoned about cultural difference and about boundaries.

Absence functions in this text to reveal the assumptions of Greek culture about itself, about its relationship to the barbarian other. The barbarians "say" themselves on stage, and in so doing delineate their opposites, the Greeks. The stage convention, the absence of the Hellenes, establishes an implicit polarity, as well as a subtle identification of the audience with their Persian enemies,

Kaineus and Centaurs, Seventh Century B.C.

Achilles and Penthesilea,
British Museum. *(Courtesy
of Trustees of the
British Museum.)*

Athenian Treasury at
Delphi

Athenian Treasury at
Delphi

Centauromachy at
Olympia

Centauromachy, Par-
thenon metope, British
Museum. *(Courtesy
of Trustees of the British
Museum.)*

Centaur/Lapith Duel, Parthenon Metope, British Museum.
(Courtesy of Trustees of the British Museum.)

Parthenon Frieze, British Museum. *(Courtesy of Trustees of the British Museum.)*

Artemis and Apollo Arriving at the Centauromachy, Bassae Frieze, British Museum. *(Courtesy of Trustees of the British Museum.)*

Centaurs Attacking Lapiths, Bassae Frieze, British Museum. *(Courtesy of Trustees of the British Museum.)*

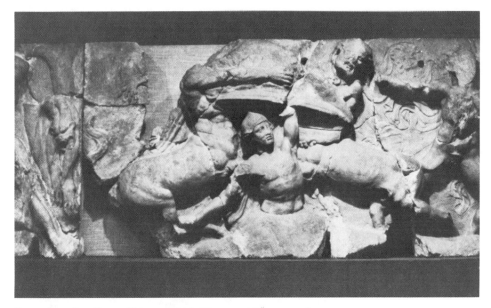

Centauromachy, Bassae Frieze, British Museum. *(Courtesy of Trustees of the British Museum.)*

Centaurs with Heads and Torsos of Old Men, Bassae Frieze, British Museum. *(Courtesy of Trustees of the British Museum.)*

Amazonomachy, Bassae Frieze, British Museum. *(Courtesy of Trustees of the British Museum.)*

Amazonomachy, Bassae Frieze, British Museum. *(Courtesy of Trustees of the British Museum.)*

Herakles Panel, Bassae Frieze, British Museum. *(Courtesy of Trustees of the British Museum.)*

who are seen as if in a distorting mirror, both hauntingly similar and radically other.

The *Persae* is based throughout on the notion of separation. War, *polemos*, enacts this separation articulated through battle, establishing polar opposites within the category of the human. Through the means of the battle of Salamis, division is effected between Greek and barbarian. The form of the tragedy repeats, re-enacts ritually this division by showing the Persians alone, *separated* from the Greeks. In fact, as H.D. Broadhead points out in his edition of the text, the presence of the Ionian Greeks among the Persian troops, fighting against the Athenians, is carefully suppressed in the parodos of the *Persae.*[15]

The barbaric language of the Persian chorus, their listing of the names of the Persian horde, stress the difference, expressed clearly here, between them and their Hellene foe. In the first two lines of the parodos the chorus names the two antagonists, and thus marks the separation which is to characterize the tragedy as a whole:

> "Of the Persians gone
> To the land of Greece
> here are the trusted. . . ."

$$[1-2]^{16}$$

The two "races" are named, and the initial situation of the drama, the absence of the Persian army from its proper place, at home, establishes the central theme of separation. Persians, different from Greeks in language and in homeland, have tried to upset the proper order of things by their invasion of Hellas, by attempting to unite two peoples which must remain separate.

The metaphor of the yoke, *zugon*, resounds through the play and clarifies Aeschylus' views on the appropriate relationship between Greek and barbarian, one of distinct separation.[17] The metaphor touches on ideas of political and social institutions. It is introduced with an allusion to the slavish yoke, *zugon . . . doulion*, (50), which the Persian army seeks to throw over Hellas. The image is repeated at line 72, where the chorus describes Xerxes' bridge over the Hellespont as the casting round of a yoke on the neck of the deep. Xerxes has sought to enslave land and sea like animals or slaves. At this moment, the elders celebrate his attempt, adorning their song with the exotic names of the Persian warriors.

Atossa's prophetic dream, which she recounts to the chorus in her first appearance, extends the notion of the yoke as an allegorical enslavement:

> "Two women as an apparition came,
> One in Persian robes instructed well,
> The other Doric, both in splendor dressed,
> Who grand and most magnificent excelled
> Us now, their beauty unreproached, spotless;
> Sisters [*kasignêta genous/tautou*] they, who casting for their
>   fathers' land,
> She Greece received, she Asia, where to dwell.
> Then strife arose between them, or so I dreamed;
> And my son, observing this, tries to check
> And soothe them; he yokes [*zeugnusin*] them to a chariot,
> Bridles their necks: and one, so arrayed, towers
> Proud, her mouth obedient to reins;
> But the other stamps, annoyed, and rends apart
> Her trappings in her hands; unbridled, seizes
> The car and snaps its yoke [*zugon*] in two . . ."
>
> [181-196]

Atossa includes all mankind in the doublet Greeks and Persians.[18] She sees the two nations as females to be yoked together by a male.

The doublet Greek and barbarian is like the doublet land and sea. G.E.R. Lloyd says, "we find couplets often used instead of single inclusive terms *to express a general notion.* The pair 'land and sea,' for example, is used to refer to the whole earth."[19]

> Greek writers seem to have had a special fondness for coupling terms in this way, using opposites as points of reference by which to indicate a class as a whole or to mark distinctions within one, and sometimes we find that *both* opposite terms are mentioned when *only one* is strictly relevant.[20]

In fact, in the *Persae* as a whole, we find rather that one opposite term is stressed throughout, when both are relevant and present by an implied opposition. Only barbarians speak; their words evoke the existence of their polar opposites, the Greeks, while at the same time exciting the audience's sympathy toward a tentative dissolution of polarity.

At another moment in the play, Atossa tries to gain some understanding of the Greeks and questions the chorus of elders about them. Throughout the early part of the tragedy, the chorus of *pistoi* stress the golden wealth of the Persian empire (in the parodos alone they mention the *poluchrusôn hedranôn* (3-4), *poluchrusou stratias* (9), *poluchrusoi Sardeis* (45), *Babulôn d'/hê poluchrusos, chru/sogonou geneas* (80).)[21] In contrast here, Athens is described for Atossa as the city of silver:

"Their earth is veined with silver treasuries." [*argurou pêgê tis autois esti, thêsauros chthonos.*]

[238]

This opposition prepares the way for the further remarks of the queen, who proves conveniently ignorant concerning the Athenians. The chorus' descriptions work on the oppositions gold/silver, bow/lance, slavery/freedom. The queen asks:

"Who commands them? Who is shepherd of their host [*poimanôn*]?"

[241]

The chorus responds:

"They are slaves to none, nor are they subject."

[242]

The polarization between the two peoples is strengthened by Atossa's incredulity; the focus is not necessarily on the difference between the two armies, but rather on the habits of mind of the Persian as opposed to those of the Greek audience. The Persian queen's natural reflex is to inquire about wealth, then about weapons, then about the character of the opponent's despot. She is incapable of understanding the way of life of the Greeks, and in this she reveals her barbarian nature.

The play's Persian characters seem to accept and elaborate the barbarian/Greek opposition, casting a portrait in the negative of Greek culture and character, revealing Xerxes' error as a failure to respect difference. In her dream, Atossa sets her son apart from the doublet in an ideologically significant gesture. The King, *basileus*, is outside the inclusive polarity and as an external term is seen as mediator by Atossa. Since she does not consider him to be contained within the opposition represented by the two sisters, he properly attempts to establish peace and to yoke together the doublet, the all-inclusive polarity, under his domination. The effect of Atossa's dream is to reveal her inability to distinguish between these two "kinds" and their necessary separation. The force of the moment is lost if one simply reads the Hellenic sister as Aeschylus' idea of the Greeks; the representation works at a more complex level of distancing.

Another barbaric, false idea of Atossa's is her assumption that the Greek nation, like that of the Persians, is female and therefore naturally to be overpowered and linked by the male king. The Greeks would adjust the polarity and insist again and again, in a slur that would be repeated, that the Eastern peoples, the barbarians, Trojan, Persian, were weak, impotent, and effeminate, and that the manliness, the virility of the Western nation was *naturally* opposed to the barbarian character.[22] And finally Atossa makes an association between these two sisters and the animals of a team, in the metaphor of yoking. The fact that Atossa speaks of harnessing, reining Greece and Persia together, like horses drawing a chariot, demonstrates her inability to imagine real freedom from domination.

Her son shares her vision. Xerxes' crime was a failure to maintain the distinction between polar opposites, an attempt to join irreconcilable terms and remain outside as the dominating figure over both. His father, sorrowing over his son's *hubris*, points out that Xerxes blurred the separation between land and sea. This violation of natural boundaries is assimilated to his political error; one can no more link Greek and barbarian into a single team than one can harness land and sea together. The yoke of the mortal barbarian will be shaken off by the sea, by Poseidon, just as it will be resisted by the other, the nation of Hellenes:

> "The spring I of evil's found: my son in ignorance
> Discovered it, by youthful pride; who hoped
> To check the sacred waters of the Hellespont
> By chains [*desmômasin*], just as if it were a slave. He smoothed
> His way, yoking Neptune's flowing Bosphorus
> With hammered shackles. Mortal though he was,
> By folly thought to conquer [*kratêsein*] all the gods
> And Neptune."

[744-750]

Difference, expressed in polarities, is represented as natural and must be respected; the attempt to set oneself outside and above the Greek/barbarian difference is an attempt to assimilate oneself to the first term of the immortal/mortal polarity, and must be punished. *Hubris* bears a crop of *atê* (821-2), in the inevitable and natural progression of the seasons.

The unnatural quality of the yoke Xerxes attempted to impose is emphasized by the tragedian. The yoke which was carried by *polemos* served not to link the two kinds of mortals into a single team; it served rather as the occasion for a clarification of their difference. Posed against the unnatural yoking of war is the natural union of marriage, also referred to as a yoke by Aeschylus. Here the proper partner is a woman of one's own kind. In their elaborate parodos, the chorus of elders refers to the Persian woman bereft of her mate:

> "Beds with longing [*pothô*] fill with tears,
> Persian wives in softness weep;
> Each her armèd furious lord
> Dismissed with gentle love and grief,
> Left all alone in the yoke [*monozux*]."

[133-139]

The verse ends emphatically; the Persian wife is alone in her harness, *monozux*. Marriage and the marriage-bed are the proper site of the yoke in which man and woman of the same kind are bound together. The situation of war destroys this relationship and merely strengthens ideas of racial difference rather than obliterating them. Again at line 542, Aeschylus reiterates the metaphor of marriage as a yoking together of male and female:

"Ladies of Persia
Softly are weeping
Desiring each
Him to behold
Wedded but lately [artizugian],
Couches forsaking
Soft as their coverlets
(Youth was voluptuous)
Their sorrows, insatiate woe."

[541-545]

The marriage yoke, when broken by war, brings desire and yearning for the yoke-mate.[23] The natural pairing of the marital bed is contrasted with the unnatural attempt by Xerxes to yoke together land and sea, Hellene and Persian. War, the polar opposite of *philia*, of marital conjunction, is a temporary *agôn* which must end by affirming difference.

Darius, father of Xerxes and bearer of an extra weight of wisdom because he comes from the dead, is praised by the chorus for his earlier sovereignty over the Persian nation. His reign did not suffer from the excesses of Xerxes'; he never attempted to achieve the status of a god, to force the unnatural union of continents through war. Darius conquered the Ionian cities, the islands off the coast, but without moving himself from his proper place. He won the chorus' praise and nostalgia for an understanding of his own limitations:

"For many the cities he sacked never crossing the Halys,
Nor leaving his hearth [hestias] in a rush."

[864-866]

The good man stays at his hearth, stays in his own marriage bed.[24] Xerxes, who leaves his palace to invade the territory of the

Hellenes, is punished by the gods themselves for his unwillingness to recognize difference and the necessity for separation of kinds.

The *Persae* ends with the desperate lamentations of the king and his subjects, who return to their homes. The sympathy of the Greek audience for their agonies is evoked in this extended scene through the common experience of suffering during the terrible war. Greeks and barbarians suffer in common, as human beings. The tragedy threatens to dissolve their opposition in a moment of shared lamentation.

Yet in fact, the right balance has ultimately been restored, to the Persians' sorrow. The Athenian audience, while sympathizing with their pain, can nonetheless rejoice at the resolution:[25] The Persians are set at their own hearths, Xerxes is once again at home, ready to dominate his slavish subjects. War, the agonistic confrontation, has served only momentarily to test, finally to reaffirm the polarity Greeks/barbarians, as natural as that between land and sea, gods and men.

Polemos here sets Greek against alien, and clarifies their difference. In a similar way the figures on early classical metopes oppose one another—Greek and Amazon, Greek hero—Herakles or Theseus—and monster or highwayman. The agonistic relationship both defines them in opposition to each other and shows them acting out their enmity. The early classical temple, decorated with metopes, defined the nature of the cosmos in terms of a series of polarities which are analogous to each other. Herakles battling Geryon is analogous to Theseus fighting Sciron. Similarly, the characters and chorus of Aeschylus' drama speak through polarizing doublets, breaking the world up into mutually exclusive couplets—land/sea, mortal/immortal, Greek/barbarian. The tragedy represents one side of the *agôn* at the moment after defeat, when the possibility of identity is strong, yet insists once again on separation of kinds, on the division of the field of action. As on a metope, there is opposition between two distinct beings, naturally separated from one another. There is no higher order of man, no king or father. War is the process, the occasion which illuminates the relationship of polarity. The form of the *Persae* involves an almost compulsive separation between Greeks and Persians, one which paradoxically threatens to dissolve into identity yet which finally keeps the barbarian at a distance, polarized spatially in his difference from the Hellene.

The injunction on representing current history is operating here; in this case the political danger of direct representation is clear.[26] If Aeschylus were to show the hero of Salamis on the tragic stage, it would be an overly explicit political statement within the party struggles of the day.[27] He would be aligning himself indirectly with the Themistoclean party.

Yet in the very exposition of the situation of the Persians, there is a counter-current, a contradiction suggested earlier which exposes the impossibility of separation. By bringing Susa to the tragic *skênê*, by having Athenian actors play the parts of Xerxes, Atossa, Darius, by representing their very human concerns, Aeschylus reveals the qualities they shared with the Greeks. The Persians are "other," different, yet in their presence within the city as the tragedy was played out, they demanded another sort of recognition. They too form a closed, endogamous circle, reinforcing the notion of otherness *parallel* to Greekness in its closure. In the fourth century, Alexander was to act finally on the perception of Aeschylus, that the mighty—kings and queens—are the same in every culture.[28] Thus even within the polarity Hellene/foreigner, there is a clear appreciation of likeness, of sameness in difference, which works dialectically with the more rigid opposition enacted by the staging of the *Persae*.

Nonetheless, at this moment in the history of the democratic city, the citizen defined himself speculatively as one element of the polarity Greek/barbarian, whose place was at his hearth, at the center of the city. The definition of the subject of Aeschylean drama, of the subject of the young democracy, depended on this polarity, on the situation of the citizen in opposition to the foreign enemy. This relationship was dominant in the years after the Persian Wars, in the self-definition of the *polis*. Greek was Greek because he was not barbarian, because Greek met barbarian in war, in the *agôn* which separated, and was not yoked with him under the great king.

The series of oppositions articulated by Thales— Greek/barbarian, human/animal, man/woman—is a catalogue through which the Greek, human, male came to know himself. That self could be maintained whole and unthreatened when separation of kinds was maintained. Difference was a simple matter of articulating that series of significant oppositions. Discourse, at this stage, relied on definition through separation, through the polarization of kinds of beings. Aeschylus enacted that separation in the very form of the *Persae*.

Aeschylus' later tragedy the *Seven Against Thebes*, produced in 467, is also a drama based on oppositions; its characters live in a world defined by the differences between inside and out, male and female, land and sea. The women of Thebes, held within the circle of their city's walls, watch and wait as a series of seven hostile heroes hurls itself against them. The safety of Thebes and the fusion of the images of the ship of state and the Cadmeian land, unity of earth and sea, are effected through the mutual destruction of the sons of Oedipus, identical in their difference. Their sacrifice ensures the integrity of the city's encircling walls. The absolute separation of the *Persae*, concerned with Greek/barbarian difference, has given way to a more classical concern with life among the Greeks, who are seen as brothers locked in an agonistic relationship which must be resolved for the city to survive.

The *Oresteia*, Aeschylus' great masterpiece and the only surviving trilogy of Greek tragedy, was produced still later, in 458, and represents a very different phase in the analogical period of reasoning of the fifth century. In this magnificent drama, Aeschylus works with the polarities between Greek and barbarian, male and female, human and divine, to build an over-arching structure of progress, from the archaic, monarchical past, a world dominated by revenge and the "phallic" Clytemnestra, to a community of equals, where the vengeful, monstrous Furies are set underground, banished by the votes of the Athenians and the goddess Athena. Froma Zeitlin has shown how the richness of Aeschylus' polarizing and hierarchizing imagery creates a new misogynistic myth, in this "gynecocentric document."[29] The absolute separation of kinds revealed in the *Persae* is dialectically enriched and deepened in the course of the trilogy. The opposition between Greek and barbarian gives way to an analogical discourse on the city itself. Even as Aeschylus traces progress in social and political relations, he acts out the securing of patriarchy, the definition of marriage as the exchange of women by men. This model, which is the basis of the classical ideas of family and city, stands behind the brilliant interrogation of them later in the century in Sophocles' *Trachiniae*.

NOTES

1.   See Davis, op. cit., 450-64; and Montagu, op. cit.:

The Greeks, as also the Romans, were singularly free of anything resembling race prejudice. A study of the culture, and literatures of mankind, shows us that the conception that there are natural or biological races of mankind which differ from one another mentally as well as physically is an idea which was not developed until the latter part of the eighteenth century.

[18]

Montagu believes that the rationalizations for slavery and racism come when these institutions are under attack [16-17].

2.   For the origins of ideas on men's dark blood and the soul, see R.B. Onians, *The Origins of European Thought about the Body, the Mind, the Soul, the World, Time, and Fate* (Cambridge, 1951). See also Lloyd, op. cit., p. 16; and F.M. Snowden, *Blacks in Antiquity, Ethiopians in the Greco-Roman Experience* (Cambridge, Mass., 1970).

3.   See J.E. Powell, *A Lexicon to Herodotus*, 2nd ed., (Hildesheim, 1960), under *barbaros*, p. 58. On Herodotos, see Pembroke, op. cit.; C.W. Fornara, *Herodotus, An Interpretative Essay* (Oxford, 1971); H.R. Immerwahr, *Form and Thought in Herodotus* (Cleveland, 1966); Seth Benardete, *Herodotean Inquiries* (The Hague, 1969), on Herodotus and the Amazons, pp. 118-119; and Hartog, op. cit.

4.   Baldry, op. cit., pp. 21 ff.

5.   See, for example, G.S. Kirk, ed., *Language and Background of Homer* (Cambridge, 1964), *passim*.

6.   Vernant, *Mythe et pensée*, pp. 151 ff.

7.   Arès et Aphrodite, *Polemos* et *Philia*, *Neikos* et *Harmonia*, *Eris* et *Eros*, peuvent ainsi apparaître dans les structures du panthéon, les récits légendaires, les théories des philosophes, comme des couples de puissances opposées mais étroitement unies, présidant à ces institutions complémentaires que forment la guerre et le mariage aussi longtemps que la vengeance privée et l'échange des femmes s'exercent dans la même cadre de relations interfamiliales.

Ibid., p. 33. Vernant argues that this complementarity of war and marriage disappears with the city [39], while on the contrary I believe on the level of mythic structures, the basis of tragic drama, this complementarity survives and is one of the issues addressed in the tragic texts of the democracy.

8.   Guthrie, op. cit., pp. 77 ff.

9.   See, for example, Richmond Lattimore, *Story Patterns in Greek Tragedy* (Ann Arbor, 1964), where he remarks the absence of any situation of choice in the *Persae* [36].

10.   Kirk and Raven, op. cit., #215.

11.   Albin Lesky, *Greek Tragedy*, trans. by H.A. Frankfort (London and New York, 1965), pp. 51-52.

12.   Ibid., p. 50. Lesky calls Phrynichus' work "historical drama," and adds:

> The curtailment of historical drama's development may have saved tragedy from a dangerous possibility. We have already denied that the link between Phrynichus' historical dramas and Themistocles was accidental. . . . We can see here a potential development which would have led away from the deep, genuine bond between tragedy and city-state which existed in the case of Aeschylus.
>
> [52]

See also H.W. Smyth, *Aeschylean Tragedy* (Berkeley, 1924), pp. 69-79.

13.   Helen Bacon, *Barbarians in Greek Tragedy* (New Haven, 1961).

14.   See the forthcoming study on Aeschylus by Froma Zeitlin, and her brilliant essay on the *Oresteia*: "The Dynamics of Misogyny: Myth and Mythmaking in the *Oresteia*," *Arethusa* 11.1, 2 (Spring and Fall 1978): 149-84:

> For Aeschylus, civilization is the ultimate product of conflict between opposing forces, achieved not through a *coincidentia oppositorum* but through a hierarchization of values. The solution, therefore, places Olympian over chthonic on the divine level, Greek over barbarian on the cultural level, and male over female on the social level. But the male-female conflict subsumes the other two. . . .
>
> [149]

15.   H.D. Broadhead, *The Persae of Aeschylus* (Cambridge, 1960), p. 44. See also the extensive bibliography, xi-xiv.

16.   All translations of the Greek tragedians' works are from *The Complete Greek Tragedies*, ed. by David Grene and Richmond

Lattimore (Chicago, 1959). *The Persians* was translated by Seth G. Benardete.

17. On the use of metaphor in Aeschylus, see F.R. Earp, *The Style of Aeschylus* (New York, 1948), pp. 99 ff.; on the yoke, W.B. Stanford, *Aeschylus in His Style* (Dublin, 1942), p. 96; E.T. Owen, *The Harmony of Aeschylus* (Toronto, 1952), p. 25.

18. On the yoking, scourging, and passage over the Hellespont, see Herodotus 6.35-36.55. "The proudly harnessed Persian woman represents the compliantly feminine Id-component of Atossa's counter-oedipal complex," according to George Devereux, *Dreams in Greek Tragedy* (Berkeley and Los Angeles, 1976), p. 17.

19. Lloyd, op. cit., p. 91.

20. Ibid., p. 92.

21. R.P. Winnington-Ingram, defends this "repetitive verbal technique in Aeschylus," in "A Word in *The Persae*," *Bulletin of the University of London Institute of Classical Studies* 20 (1973), 38.

22. In an ironic twist, the Romans turned the characterization against the Greeks; see, for example, Juvenal's *Graeculus*, 3.78.

23. Broadhead calls *artizugian* "a choice instance of abstract for concrete," op. cit., p. 145.

24. For the implied contrast with Xerxes, see Broadhead, ibid., p. 217.

25. Peter Walcot inaccurately calls this "jingoism," in *Greek Drama in its Theatrical and Social Context* (Cardiff, 1976), p. 96.

26. See Podlecki, op. cit., pp. 8-26.

27. Vernant, "Ambiguity and Reversal . . ."

28. Tarn, op. cit.

29. Zeitlin, op. cit., p. 150.

IV

Humans and Animals

If the structure of the *Persae*, describing one side of the agôn of the Persian Wars, evokes that of the early classical metopes, it is not surprising, since the literary and artistic texts share a notion of difference based on the polarization of kinds. In this chapter I will look at another such polarity, the human/animal doublet, the second of the terms by which Thales defined himself. The problem is altered, in that the criterion of difference is no longer separation, the geographical particularity of Greeks and barbarians, as it was in Aeschylus' early work. A text like the *Trachiniae*, the focus of this chapter, treats the problematic of differentiation not as definition through oppositions, but centers rather on the central figure in the *polis*, the human subject, the man who exchanges women within the city. The *polis* is the terrain of his existence, and he acts out his life within its circumference, keeping his enemies, animals as well as barbarians, the alien and the monstrous, at bay outside the circle of exchange.

Those who date the *Trachiniae* to the 440s are convincing, although others question judgements based on purely stylistic features, or supposed references to other tragedies.[1] If indeed the *Trachiniae* was produced in the same decades as the Parthenon sculptures, these works share a concern with community, with the limits within which social life can occur. After the Greeks' victory over the Persians, the Athenians in particular enjoyed prosperity and stability which led to Athens' dominance in the Aegean under the guidance of Pericles. The greatest tragedies, the high classical temples, reveal the Athenians' vivid imagination, their rich intellectual life, and the tensions which arose in a restricted community attempting to assert power over others.

The problematic articulated by the *Trachiniae* is analogous to that enacted on the Parthenon, where the city engages in its ritual continuously, eternally, within the colonnade, while the metopes represent enemies at the boundaries, fixed in opposition and held there in the archaic past through the martial courage of the Greek youths. Like Centaurs and Amazons, the barbarians are held outside the circle of ritual represented in the Panathenaia. The bestial, violent, chaotic figures of myth are made analogous to the enemies, recently defeated, who held the center of the stage in Aeschylus' tragedy. Here they are exiled, placed on the outside to define the farthest boundaries within which the city inscribes itself.

The very process of tragedy comes to center on man within the city, elaborating his relations to other men like him. The gods become distant figures. The *Trachiniae* focuses on man, on the marital exchange which founds culture, on the necessity for endogamy among citizens. It is different from the *Persae* in that the enemy is no longer represented as far distant, separate in its isolation from the other. In the *Trachiniae* the bestial threatens to intervene into the most central institution founding the city, the orderly exchange of women through marriage.[2] The pattern of reasoning has altered, although it still proceeds through polarity and analogy; analysis has shifted from a catalogue of self/other to a focus on the self, on the Greek human male, centered on himself in interaction with those like him. The other is now relegated to the edge of culture. The articulation of *polis* culture, of social relations within, has become necessary and requires the expulsion of the different—barbarian and animal.

There are other tragedies which touch on animal-human difference—the *Bacchae*, for example, displays the ways in which men and women, and gods, can take on the aspects of animals. A Bacchante likens herself to a fawn, Dionysos is a bull in the eyes of Pentheus. Yet the *Trachiniae* is an especially enlightening text for the problem with which I am concerned here, since it considers not only the bestial qualities of man, but those very mediate beings discussed above, the Centaurs. One of the absent yet significant characters of the drama is the Centaur Nessos.

The issue of animal/human boundaries, in the form of metamorphosis, is introduced in the first speech of the *Trachiniae*, as Deianeira fearfully recounts her sexual history:

"While I still lived in Pleuron, with Oeneus my father,
I conceived an agonizing fear of marriage.
No other Aetolian woman ever felt such fear,
for my suitor was the river Acheloüs,
who used to come to ask my father for my hand,
taking three forms - first, clearly a bull, and then
a serpent with shimmering coils, then a man's body
but a bull's face. . . ."[3]

[9-14]

Herakles saved Deianeira from this monster, as the chorus reminds the audience (497).

The play works throughout on these themes of opposition among mortal men, gods, and bizarre hybrid animals. Herakles is continually set against opponents from the world of gods or animals; his labors consist of an endless series of such encounters. The playwright uses military and agonistic language to describe the numerous confrontations.[4] In the tightly compressed epode of lines 519-522, the metaphor implicit in *klimakes*, wrestling holds (520), figures in the synaesthetic, rapid force of this passage in a way reminiscent of the innumerable scenes of Herakles battling his enemies on metopes and vases of the classical period (cf. 441-2). There too the hero is pitted against a single enemy, one with inhuman, super-bestial characteristics, in an intense, abbreviated *agôn*.

Herakles rescued Deianeira, who waited on a hill far away, as he later saved his bride from the unwelcome attentions of another hybrid creature, the horse/man Nessos. Deianeira recalls:

"I too was carried on his shoulders when my father
sent me to follow Heracles for the first time
as his wife. When I was halfway across
his hands touched me lustfully [*mataiais chersin*]."

[562-65]

Passed from father to husband, Deianeira is almost taken by this violent creature, who displays the characteristic brutality of the Centaurs as they are portrayed in art. His violence is accentuated and made more threatening to the human woman because he is a

hybrid, cross-species creature. The bestial, heightened masculinity
of the Centaurs is re-emphasized in this episode.

Once again Herakles snatched Deianeira from the lustful
advances of an inhuman being; this time however, the world
against which Herakles constantly defines himself, the world of
bi-form, tri-form, archaic monsters, has marked the woman, and
will return in time to destroy him. The dying Centaur, struck by
Herakles' arrow, counseled Deianeira:

> "If you take in your hands this blood, clotted in
> my wounds, wherever it is black with the bile
> of the Hydra, the monstrous serpent [*thremma*] of Lerna, in
>   which
> he dipped his arrows, you will have a charm [*kêlêtêrion*] over
> the heart of Heracles, so he will never look
> at another woman and love her more than you."
>
> [572-577]

The unguent is a mingling of the Hydra's blood with that of the
Centaur; another version of the myth said that the potion included
the sperm of Nessos.[5]

Herakles saved his wife from rape by the Centaur and killed
the beast for his attempt. Yet the tragedy traces the consequences
of Nessos' violation of Deianeira. The Centaur, in laying his
hands on her, broke into the circle of human exchange of women
and caused disaster to the house of Herakles. His intervention
leads to the death of both the violated woman and her husband.
Deianeira preserves the mark of the Centaur on her:

> "I neglected none of the instructions that beast (*thêr*)
> the centaur explained to me, lying in agony
> with the sharp arrowhead in his side. I kept them
> like an inscription in bronze that cannot be washed away
> [*chalkês hopôs dusnipton ek deltou graphên*]."
>
> [680-683]

Deianeira becomes herself the surface for the Centaur's writing,
preserving his words to destroy her husband and herself.

Jeffrey Henderson's remarks about *Lysistrata* 151 are interesting here, since he points out that *delta* is used there, and elsewhere, "for its shape as the female pubis. . . ."[6] The pun on *deltos*, the writing tablet, is significant in that Nessos' act of violence is sexual, in that the tradition records semen as part of the love-potion Deianeira preserves, in that she stresses the dark hidden place in which she smears the potion:[7]

> "Now, when it had to do its work,
> at home, inside the house, secretly I smeared it on
> some wool, a scrap I pulled from one of the household
>   sheep,
> and then I folded my gift and put it in a chest
> before the sun could shine on it. . . ."
>
> [689-692]

Metaphorically at least, Deianeira bride of Herakles is touched and raped by the horse/man. His act of sexual violence in the past corresponds to the destruction of the hero in the present time of tragic action. Herakles put on the cloak sent to him by Deianeira, as he put on the lion's skin after conquering the beast of Nemea. This time, however, the enmity of his beastly rival survives to destroy him through the agency of the prize, Deianeira.

Although the chorus urged her not to use the remedy, the *pharmakon*, untried, Deianeira persisted in her plan to recapture Herakles' love with the unguent. In a sense her self-punishment on learning of her husband's anguish is justified, since she indeed willed his destruction, however unconsciously.[8] Her sexual fear is in evidence throughout the play, in her laments about the hideous prospect of marriage to Ach" $\bar{a}$ Acheloüs, in her description of her married life:

> "Chosen partner for the bed of Herakles [*lechos . . . kriton*],
> I nurse fear after fear [*ek phobou phobon trephô*], always wor-
>   rying
> over him. I have a constant relay of troubles;
> some each night dispels - each night brings others on."
>
> [27-30]

As Jebb points out, *lechos* (bed) equals bride, in a common metonymy. Deianeira destroys her husband, the man who substituted for the beast, in part because he treated her inhumanly, deserting her for years of beast-chasing and finally bringing back to her, when he had finally reached the *telos* of his labors, a foreign bride, a younger woman blossoming in her house.

Deianeira reveals, in her words of regret and anguish, her knowledge about the deadly poison she smeared on the robe sent to Herakles:

> "I know that arrow which struck Nessus injured even
> Chiron, who was a god, and all animals,
> whatever it touches, it kills. This same poison which seeped
> black and bloody, from the wounds of Nessus, how can
> it fail to kill Heracles too?"
>
> [714-718]

The sexual ambivalence of Greek women towards husbands is here clearly rendered by Sophocles, in Deianeira's suppression of this vital information.[9] Like Clytemnestra and Medea, she is a murderess, albeit against her conscious desires.

The potion, the *kêlêtêrion*, of the *Trachiniae* shares the characteristics of the *pharmakon* described in Jacques Derrida's essay on Plato, where the *pharmakon* is a poison, a cure, is writing, is Socrates himself.[10]

The attempted abduction of Deianeira, a contaminating act of intervention in the past, requires catharsis. Herakles' act of violence against Iole triggers the cleansing action of the *pharmakon*, the sign of past aggression. Deianeira, contaminated through her contact with Nessos, is sacrificed, expelled, along with her husband. The *oikos*, basic unit of the city, is purged through the agency of the poisonous *pharmakon*. The mixed Centaur and hydra blood, with the possible admixture of Centaur semen, functions as both a sign of pollution, and as its cure. It kills both Herakles and, indirectly, Deianeira; thus it cleanses the city of the taint brought on by the Centaur's initial act of sexual violence.

Deianeira offers up the potion as a cure for what she repeatedly calls her husband's *nosos*, his sickness, his affliction. Eros

has struck him with terrible desire, *deinos himeros* (476), which is
likened again and again to *nosos* (=Nessos):

"And yet, when he
is sick as he so often is with this same sickness [*nosô*]
I am incapable of anger."

[543-544]

The cure for Herakles' plague should be desire, this time desire
directed toward his wife Deianeira. Nessos, when he instructed
her, called the potion a *kêlêtêrion* (575), a magic charm, a spell
(cf. 554, 998). The potion should have the effect of cleansing, of
purification from his disease.

The actual effect of the *pharmakon* is the contrary; it turns
wool to dust (699) and makes the earth bubble with a substance
blue like grape-juice.[11] Herakles blames his wife for the horrible
pain he suffers as the poison begins to affect him; the chorus
accuses rather the Centaur and the Hydra, assigning guilt away
from Deianeira:

"If there clings to him in a murderous cloud [*phonia nephela*]
the Centaur's treacherous, sure trap
and his sides are soaked with venom
that Death begat and the shimmering serpent bred,
how shall he see another sun after today's
when the Hydra, horrible and monstrous [*deinotatô* . . .
      phasmati], has
soaked in? From the black-maned beast's
treacherous words there comes to torture him
a murderous confusion,
sharp points brought to burning heat
[*hupophonia* . . . *kentra epizesanta*]."

[831-840]

The *phonia nephela*, "murderous cloud" (831) may be an allusion
to Nephele, the supposed ancestress of all the Centaurs. The
strophe is composed in ring form, with an initial reference to
Kentaurou, thought popularly to be derived from the verb *kenteô*,
prick, goad, stab, and ending with *hupophonia* . . . *kentra*,

"murderous goads" (840), which echoes the epithet used of *nephela*. The Centaurs are a deadly kind, fit to be considered with the foul serpent form of the Hydra. Together the creatures stand for all the opponents of Herakles, the Stymphalian birds, the Cretan bull and the others who are figured so often, set against him, falling in defeat on the metopes of innumerable temples throughout the Greek world. Here at last they have their revenge.[12]

Yet paradoxically Herakles preserves the city, the community, the exchange of women, in his gift, Iole, to his son Hyllus. He keeps the female object—not Deianeira, but a younger woman to replace her—within the community of equals; she is untouched by his victorious rivals. The play acts out the testing of the boundaries of the human community, allowing the other to break in, to threaten and touch the human woman, and thus to bring about Herakles' and Deianeira's end. They are polluted and destroyed by the intervention of the man/animal, the Centaur. Yet the culture continues, since the son reluctantly receives his father's gift, his woman.

Oedipus Rex is about incest, about an excess of endogamy which ends in death and sterility, in the end of a family.[13] The *Trachiniae* considers the complementary question, the necessity for a degree of endogamy for the preservation of the city, for the reproduction of a family of like beings. It depicts a circuit of exchange—Herakles receives Deianeira from her father, saving her from falling into the hands of the monster Achelous. When she is touched by the Centaur, both she and Herakles are destroyed, through the agency of this beast/man hybrid, but Herakles preserves the tenuous link between men, the exchange of women among men, by giving his captive to his son:

god/beast/man (Acheloüs)

father-----daughter-----Herakles-----"wife"-----son
(Oineus) (Deianeira)   (Iole)   (Hyllus)

man/beast (Nessos)

In a complex and elaborated narrative, the hybrid creatures Acheloüs and Nessos are excluded from the circuit of exchange of women. Their violence marks them as outside the circuit of culture. They have the power to destroy individuals by touching them with bestiality, yet the community, with great sacrifice, survives their invasion. Like the Centaurs and Amazons on the Parthenon metopes, these beasts threaten to invade human culture and are finally repulsed by the hero. The celebratory majesty of the Parthenon expresses joy at the victory of the democratic *polis* over the barbarian outside, and the form of the sculptural program sets these enemies in their proper relation to the city. Like Nessos, they are defeated, fixed in archaic, past time, fixed in death.

Yet Sophocles reveals the terrible price paid by the hero for his efforts, in the tragic deaths of Herakles and Deianeira. The heroes of the Parthenon frieze gallop to the shrine of Athena unmarked by the battles which won the city's security. Herakles and Deianeira, however, are destroyed by the fact of invasion, by the intervention of the barbaric, the bestial, in the marriage exchange. The oration of Pericles at the funeral of Athenian soldiers in 431, as reported by Thucydides (2.35-46), reveals some of the costs the *polis* paid for the victories and wealth the citizens enjoyed. And in that same funeral oration Pericles touches on the contradictory position of women in a way which clarifies the complexity of Deianeira's role in *Trachiniae*.[14] Women are, in Pericles' city, to be neither seen, heard, nor spoken of, yet they reproduce the generations of warriors who constitute Athens.[15] Without them, there would be no Athenians going forth to do battle for the city.

Deianeira is in the tragedy both a heroic figure destroyed by her unwitting actions, and a creature made analogous to the monsters who battle with Herakles in his many labors. She has an Amazon name; unlike the bull, the birds, the Amazons, she destroys him. Deianeira, like Clytemnestra, is a murderess even though she is the agent of another, the Centaur, the barbarian other whose attack on civilization was an attempt to gain power over her. In her act of unconscious violence, she becomes a figure analogous to him, not simply a victim but an agent of destruction and barbaric chaos.

The tragedy shows the attempt of civilization to construct a circle within which culture exists, from which all elements of otherness, of difference, are excluded. Yet that attempt is fated to fail in part because women, who are to be exchanged between men as a marker of that culture, approach the status of the other within. Men's hope is that women will remain silent possessions, tokens of exchange, Lévi-Strauss' "words." As Deianeira acts, however, she begins to play out the impossibility, the tragic contradictions implicit in a civilization which excluded women from humanness and made them both invisible and analogous to animals.

Part of the terrible effect of the philter, the mixture, is that Herakles, defeated by a woman, in death becomes a woman:

"Neither the spear of battle, nor the army of
the earth-born giants, nor the violence of beasts [thêrion bia],
nor Greece, nor any place of barbarous tongue [aglôssas],
    not all
the lands I came to purify could ever do this.
A woman, a female, in no way like a man
[gunê de, thêlus phusa kouk andros phusin]
She alone without even a sword has brought me down."
                                            [1058-1063]

Herakles lists soldiers, giants, beasts, Greeks and barbarians, and ends with gunê, woman, in an emphatic position in the line which stresses heavily the fact, most repellent to the hero, that his final, victorious opponent substitutes for all other opponents.[16] A few lines later, he speaks of the final transformation brought about through the agency of the Centaur's pharmakon:

"Pity me,
for I seem pitiful to many others, crying
and sobbing like a girl [hôste parthenos]. . . .
Now in my misery I am discovered a woman [thêlus]."
                                            [1071-2, 1075]

He looks out from his veil like a dead man, like a bride. The hero defined himself, and an ideal of heroism, in agonistic relationship to the "others" of the Greek world, beasts and barbarians. Here at last he is faced with an even more deadly opponent, woman, who turns him into her own kind with the help of the beast. The Centaur stretches from Hades (1162), with the help of his fellow victim the Hydra, and together with the woman they destroy the son of Zeus.

Especially in the work of the greatest of the tragedians, Sophocles, the tragic hero is the locus of the collapse of traditional polarities. Just as Herakles is beast and woman, so Oedipus, as Vernant argues, is less than a man, a *pharmakos*, and more than a man, a godlike king. Tragedy reveals with great clarity the polarizing logic of the Greek thinkers of the fifth century, at the same time as it puts that logic into question by representing the heroes as liminal, paradoxical figures. At critical moments in the best of tragedies, as in this scene of Herakles' death, there is a fusion of oppositions, a released dialectic, which plays upon the audience's pity and fear, and demands an examination of the traditional categories of difference. As the fifth century progresses, these moments are more intensely realized; the absolute boundaries between kinds are seen as inadequate.

The *Trachiniae* thus operates at two levels, both celebrating and collapsing boundaries. First, it enacts a definition of the center through the preservation of human women within the *polis*, for their own kind. The bride, whose identity is rendered insignificant, is passed from father to suitor, from father to son, and is kept inside the human community. Rape, the violation of ordered exchange, destroys the particular actors of the tragedy, yet leaves untouched the founding act of exchange. In this reading, Deianeira is the innocent agent, and victim, of a necessary cleansing process. She is touched by the beast and thus purification demands that both she and her husband be excised from the community of humans, while the line of exchange is sustained through the union of Hyllus and Iole. Invasion from outside is answered by catharsis. Difference is shut outside the boundaries of the metaphorical city.

However, Deianeira is not simply the token of exchange, not simply a tainted object passing between father and suitor. She becomes a central actor in the drama, and by analogy is associated with the enemies of Herakles, with Centaur, Hydra, Amazon. Thus the possibility of destruction of the city from within is introduced, and the posture of vigilance by the Greek hero, on the metopes, is revealed as insufficient. Difference may perhaps be hidden within the *polis*, in the contradictory and ambiguous situation of women. The model of the circle, with enemies at its boundaries, is explored by Sophocles. Its tensions are revealed in the analogical process which links Deianeira to the foes of Herakles. The confidence and euphoria of the city in its moment of victory are sustained only through great sacrifice.[17] If marriage were to be a relationship between men and women, rather than the exchange of women by equal men, then it could no longer be seen as the complementary and polar opposite to *polemos*, war. The metaphor of marriage-as-culture, of the Greek man as the only actor in marriage as in war, begins to reveal stresses inside the city. The process of clarification of difference could not operate simply on the level of analogy. Sophocles' genius exposes, at the height of the city's glory, the contradictions in the city's definition of itself.

NOTES

1.   On the date of the *Trachiniae*, see E.-R. Schwinge, *Die Stellung der Trachinierinnen in Werk des Sophokles,* "Hypomnemata" I (Göttingen, 1962); Gordon Kirkwood, *A Study of Sophoclean Drama* (Ithaca, 1958), Appendix I, pp. 289-94; H.D.F. Kitto, "Sophocles, Statistics, and the *Trachiniae,*" *AJP* 1939: 178-94; and H. Siess, "Chronolog. Unters. in den Trag. des Soph." *WS* 1914: 244-95 and 1915, 27-62.

2.   See the two recent and important essays on the *Trachiniae* by Charles Segal, "Mariage et sacrifice dans les *Trachiniennes* de Sophocle," *AC* 44 (1975): 30-53, and "Sophocles' *Trachiniae*: myth, poetry, and heroic values," *YCS* (1977): 99-158; and his *Tragedy and Civilization, An Interpretation of Sophocles* (Cambridge, Mass., 1981). While I agree with much of the argument Segal makes, my reading of the play focuses less on the play as a literary text, and more on the cultural assumptions about species and sexual difference which the tragedy explores. In the later essay, Segal includes an extensive bibliography of scholarship concerning this insufficiently appreciated tragedy. A.J.A. Waldock, for example, calls the *Trachiniae* "Sophoclean Melodrama," in *Sophocles the Dramatist* (Cambridge, 1951), pp. 80 ff.

3.   *The Trachiniae* was translated by Michael Jameson.

4.   R.C. Jebb, *Sophocles, The Plays and Fragments*, vol. 5, The *Trachiniae* (Cambridge, 1892). On the Nessos episode, see Bacchylides Dith. 15.

5.   Apollodorus. 2.7.6.6; Diodorus 4.36.5; see also Dorothea Wender, "The Will of the Beast: Sexual Imagery in the *Trachiniae*" *Ramus* 3 (1974): 1-17.

6.   Henderson, op. cit., p. 146. He adds " '*delta*' is used elsewhere in literature for its shape as the female pubis . . . and in cults in the form of triangular clay votive-offerings shaped to resemble the female parts."

7.   See also Pietro Pucci on Pandora:

> . . . when the space between good and evil does not guarantee any 'exclusion of evil, the woman, the *kakon*, the difference, must be mastered: and it can be mastered, in the intention of the text, by appropriating it. Man seizes her as a booty, teaches her his ways, and forces upon her his control, his imprint, and his signature.

Op. cit., p. 113. Deianeira shows the imprinting of another master, the alien Centaur. For another statement of the connection between writing and the sexual act, note G.C. Spivak: "The hymen is the always folded (therefore never single or simple) space in which the pen writes its dissemination," introduction to Jacques Derrida, *Of Grammatology*, trans. by C.G. Spivak (Baltimore, 1976), p. lxvi.

8.   But see Jebb, in his introduction, who calls Deianeira "one of the most delicately beautiful creations in literature," op. cit., pp. xxxi, and 10; for a summary of various readings, see Oddone Longo, *Commento Linguistico alle Trachinie de Sofocle* (Padua, 1968), p. 33.

9.   On the question of Greek misogyny, especially in tragedy, and the Greek family structure, see Philip Slater, *The Glory of Hera: Greek Mythology and the Greek Family* (Boston, 1968), which should be read with the illuminating review by Helene Foley, "Sex and State in Ancient Greece," *Diacritics* (Winter 1975): 31-36.

10.   Jacques Derrida, "La pharmacie de Platon," in *La dissémination* (Paris, 1972), pp. 71-197. On Herakles, Archeloüs, and Nessos, see Joseph Fontenrose, *Python, A Study of Delphic Myth and Its Origins* (Berkeley and Los Angeles, 1959).

11.   Ezra Pound translates the passage thus:

"It had got warm
and just crumbled away, like sawdust
where somebody had been sawing a board,
but mixed up with bubbles
like the fat scum that slops over from the wine-press."

Sophokles, *Women of Trachis, A Version by Ezra Pound* (New York, 1957), pp. 30-31.

12.   J.C. Kamerbeek notes that "diseases are often thought of as beings (demons or beasts) feeding on the sufferer." *The Plays of Sophocles, Commentaries,* part II, *The Trachiniae* (Leiden, 1959), p. 181. See also "The Disease Theme in Sophocles' *Ajax, Philoctetes,* and *Trachiniae,*" *CP* 61 (1966): 223-35, and Hugh Lloyd-Jones, "Notes on Sophocles' *Trachiniae*" *YES* 22 (1972): 264-5.

13.   See the much-criticized essay of Lévi-Strauss, "The Structural Study of Myth," along with Peradotto, op. cit., Turner, op. cit., Vernant, "Oedipe sans Complexe," *Mythe et Tragédie,* pp. 75 ff.

14.   On the reproduction of the warriors, 2.44.3. On the funeral oration, see Nicole Loraux, *L'Invention d'Athènes. Histoire de l'oraison funèbre dans 'la cité classique'* (Paris, The Hague, New York, 1981.)

15.   If I am to speak also of womanly virtues [*gunaikeias . . . aretês*] referring to those of you who will henceforth be in widowhood, I will sum up all in a brief admonition: Great is your glory if you fall not below the standard which nature has set for your sex, and great also is hers of whom there is least talk among men whether in praise or in blame.

[2.45.2]

Thucydides, with an English translation by C.F. Smith, 4 vols., (Cambridge, Mass., and London [Loeb], 1951).

16.   On women in Sophocles, see T.B.L. Webster, *An Introduction to Sophocles,* 2nd ed., (London, 1969), pp. 56 ff. See also Kirkwood op. cit., pp. 110 ff. On Deianeira's heroism, C. Whitman, *Sophocles, A Study of Heroic Humanism* (Cambridge, Mass., 1951), pp. 116-19, and Gennaro Perrotta, *Sofocle* (Messina, 1935), p. 501.

17.   Victor Ehrenberg remarks:

It is possible to see in Heracles in the *Trachiniae* and, in a different way, in Odysseus in *Philoctetes,* characters reflecting the great individualistic movement which eventually proclaimed the law of the *Herrenmensch,* the doctrine of amorality and egotism which produced men such as Callicles and Alcibiades.

Sophocles and Pericles (Oxford, 1954), p. 145. See also, on Sophocles' response to the sophists, Peter Rose's essay "Sophocles' *Philoctetes* and the Teachings of the Sophists," *HSCP* 80 (1976): 49-105.

V

Men and Women

The metope is a graphic representation of the *agôn*, the confrontation between two kinds of beings seen by the Greeks as utterly different, polar opposites. War, *polemos*, is the proper relation between such creatures; it clarifies their difference and asserts the selfhood of the maker of the work of art, the citizen architect, not-barbarian, not-animal, not-female. The representations of the Greek male warrior, in combat with Centaur and Amazon, celebrate the subject of history, the victor of the Persian Wars, as does Aeschylus' tragedy the *Persae*. When the attention of the *polis* moves away from the polar opposite, the barbarian enemy, to the closed circle of the city, the *agora* in which citizens must live together, must exchange women in order to preserve the shape of the city, its artistic and literary production changes. In the *Trachiniae* the matter of difference is posed in terms of exclusion, and the problematic is not only the delimitation of boundaries for the city, but also the nature of relations between equals within.[1] The model of differentiation is no longer a series of polarities, but a circle, homogeneous in ritual and exchange, which keeps difference outside and marks its boundaries with creatures from myth like the Centaur and the Amazon. However, in the work of Euripides, even though the younger playwright's work is contemporary with that of Sophocles, there is a final crisis in speculation about difference. In the *Medea*, the focus of this chapter on male/female difference, Euripides tests the limits of the analogical mode of discourse concerning sexual, species, and racial difference.[2]

Euripides presented in a clearly articulated fashion the difficulties of maintaining traditional categories of definition in the period of the Peloponnesian War. In the *Medea*, produced in 431, he centered on the male/female difference, a seemingly clearly, physically perceptible difference which was an unquestioned element of the intellectual vocabulary of the period.[3]

Myths and works of art delineated clearly the male/female polarity as one strongly marked in the culture of the Greeks.[4] Even as such mythical creatures as the Amazons seemed to question the boundaries between male and female, the myth as a whole ended by denying the viability of single-sex female culture, and by affirming the traditional pattern of exchange of women by citizen men.

The color coding of sexual difference was expressed in poetic diction as well as in painting, as Eleanor Irwin shows in *Colour Terms in Greek Poetry.*[5] Men were described in poetry as *melas*, dark, while women were *leukos*, white; "the differentiation between the sexes was very clearly marked . . ."[6] Irwin assumes the contrast "reflects a contrast between men and women with regard to their social status and functions. Men worked outdoors, women in the house; men were tough and hardy, women soft and vulnerable."[7] In Egyptian painting, in Mycenaean wall-paintings, and on archaic vases, women's flesh was shown as light, while men's was reddish-brown or black. Irwin concludes:

> The Greeks thought that a dark complexion signified manliness, including virility and such manly virtues as courage and the ability to fight well. A fair complexion, on the other hand, signified effeminacy in men.[8]

Although the convenient contrast between kinds of flesh was no longer so readily available in red-figure vase painting, and the painters abandoned the practice of differentiating between male and female eye, the male round, the latter elongated,[9] a distinction between male and female bodies continued to be made, a differentiation that went beyond the mere outline of the body. Bernard Ashmole attributes the persistent artistic motifs like the Amazonomachy to their potential for expressing sexual difference, and remarks on the contrast "between the sinewy male torsos and limbs, and the softer more rounded forms of the Amazons, who still retain their femininity in spite of the life they lead."[10]

Although these differences were strongly marked, the Greek male youth was sometimes represented with more feminine characteristics. In *Greek Homosexuality*, K.J. Dover describes a shift of tastes from the overtly masculine representation of young men, to a more effeminate ideal expressed in poetry and in painting. Fair skin, for example, apparently became a desired attribute in objects of homosexual eros.[11]

The effect of such a work as the Bassae frieze, containing an Amazonomachy as well as the Centauromachy, is to represent the same problematic male/female difference which Euripides expressed in the *Medea*. The "other," polar opposite for Aeschylus, excluded from culture by Sophocles, emerges within the city, within the closed ritual space of temple and tragic drama, to challenge the old ideas of difference and to disrupt the processes of reasoning about difference which depended on polarity and analogy. In the *Medea*, Euripides focuses on the polarization of male and female, extends the definition of the "other" to include foreigner and female, and watches as the analogy works itself out in the text.

E.M. Blaiklock, in *The Male Characters of Euripides*, points to the central tension in the *Medea*:

> The conflict between the sexes was its inspiration, and there is reason to believe that, during the Peloponnesian War, that conflict was passing through an acute stage. Some twenty years before the production of the *Medea*, a political event in Athens had done something to focus on the social problem which the status of women presented. A law had been passed restricting the citizenship to those who had Athenian parents on both sides.[12]

The play is about the conflict between the sexes. But the conflict is expressed in particular terms which draw it into the nexus of differences discussed earlier. For Medea is not simply a woman; she is bestial, alien, and female, and thus emblematic of all the differences already cited.

Early in the play, Medea laments Jason's betrayal of her, using a metaphor which illuminates the notion of differentiation in the text:

"O God, you have given mortals a sure method [*tekmêria*]
of telling the gold that is pure from the counterfeit;
Why is there no mark engraved upon men's bodies
[*oudeis charactêr empephuke sômati*]
By which we could know the true ones from the false
   ones?"[13]

             [516-519]

The word translated "mark," *charactêr*, comes from the verb
charassô, meaning "sharpen," "whet," "scratch." A *charactêr* is
a mark, an impression, a brand; it can mean a letter, a hieroglyph,
a brand on an animal or slave, the mark, the die, the impression
made on a coin. The *charactêr*, the assay-mark, distinguishes one
coin from another, shows origin, weight, and value, and reveals to
the receiver the nature of an object he touches and exchanges. In
this passage, Medea cries out for a mark born into men, an
inscription which would reveal kinds of men to sight or touch.
She has been deceived by Jason, who is counterfeit.[14]

 In the *Hippolytus*, which was produced shortly after the
Medea, there is a similar plea for signs, for marks of difference in
a world of confusion.[15] Theseus, in his quarrel with Hippolytus,
the Amazon's son, says:

"If there were
some token [*tekmêrion*] now, some mark to make the division
clear between friend and friend, the true and the false!
All men should have two voices, one the just voice,
and one as chance would have it. In this way
the treacherous scheming voice would be confuted
by the just, and we should never be deceived."

             [925-931]

Appearances, like voices, are deceiving in this new world, and
both Medea and Theseus search in vain for marks of difference,
visible or audible, to distinguish kinds of beings, true from counterfeit.[16]

 The crisis of differentiation is extended in the course of the
Medea. The distinction between male and female is no longer

clear and definitive. Jason expresses a desire to return to masculine *autarkeia*, self-sufficiency, recorded long before in Hesiod's myth of the time before Pandora's creation. He wishes that there were no need of women:

> "It would have been better far for men [*brotous*]
> To have got their children in some other way, and women
> Not to have existed. Then life would have been good.
> [*chrên . . . thêlu d'ouk einai genos*
> *choutôs an ouk ên ouden anthrôpous kakon*]."
>
> [573-575]

His words recall the myth of Pandora, the first of the *thêlu genos*, the female kind;[17] she was *kalon kakon*, a beautiful evil.[18]

Various alternative modes of reproduction had been considered by the Greeks. The birth of Erichthonios from earth, after Hephaistos spilled his sperm when Athena rejected his advances, the birth of the Centaurs from a cloud—these are examples from the world of the gods, yet they are similar to Jason's fantasy in that they seek to short-circuit the normal generative pattern of humans and to produce new life without the participation of the female.[19] Jason is advocating a society like the Centaurs', where there is no reproduction, where the sexual act between the sexes is suppressed. The hero of the tragedy desires freedom from the necessity to include women in human culture. Medea, whose name refers punningly to the sexual organs,[20] is the cause of his fantasy of autonomy.

The conflict between the sexes which the *Medea* represents in exaggerated form was one which may have been a daily reality of Greek culture. Medea, in her anger and violence, stands for other wives. In a famous speech (230-251),[21] Medea spoke for the Greek wife of the fifth century, the child-bride who had no choice in the selection of her husband, whose future was decided in her adolescence by her parents, and who spent many of her married years in the women's quarters, producing children for the family of her husband.[22] The remarks of Medea about her isolation and loneliness must have struck a note of sympathy if there were women in her audience. Her complaints point up an important aspect of the Greek woman's life, never before so clearly expressed.[23]

The social practices of the Greeks led to the segregation of young women; they were brought into the closed space of the patriarchal family to avoid the overly endogamic practice of incest. Traded from one family to another to establish lines of connection between families, they insured the perpetuation of one family line in the *polis*.[24] Yet the woman, a sign of the family's participation in the life of the city, in its practice of exchange, lived as a near exile within the house. That is why Medea's position as exile-wife is so clearly marked in the tragedy. She represents, in an extreme, exaggerated form the common fate of the Greek citizen women.[25]

This speech is followed by that in which Medea speaks of herself as *apolis*, without a city, and it is preceded by her remarks about being *xenon*, a stranger in this city. This important manifesto about the situation of the Greek woman in marriage is set in the narrative in such a way as to stress the isolation, the separateness of the woman in her own home. This is a dominant issue in the play; the focus on the woman is very different from that of the *Trachiniae*, in which Deianeira is a passive agent who reacts with despair rather than anger when her husband threatens to replace her with another woman.

The notion of marriage as the peaceful complement to war can clearly no longer be sustained by Euripides. The Peloponnesian War, which began in the year the *Medea* was first produced, meant for the Athenians a radical change in the idea of war. The agonistic relationship once typical of confrontation between Greek and barbarian had come once again to define the family of the Hellenes. War this time was to be fought not with the other outside, the Persian, but with brother Greeks, who shared a common language, common gods, common ancestors. Although Greeks had fought among themselves before, this was a war of a new form, fought with a radically different sense of space. The Greek himself had become an other, and more importantly, the other could no longer be recognized by mere appearance.

The *Medea* expresses a sense of the invasion of the city by difference. It poses the question superficially in terms of a battle between the sexes, but the question of difference is extended to subsume all other categories in the analogy—barbarian and animal as well as female.[26] Medea is at the center of the tragedy; she is the figure on whom the text focuses. She is emblematic of all difference, difference which can no longer be kept at bay on the boundaries of culture, at the Hellespont, on the metopes of the Parthenon. The boundaries had broken down in war, in marriage.

Even though she is a Greek bride, civilized by her contact with Jason, Medea's barbarism is emphasized from the very first lines of the play. The nurse retraces the voyage of the Argo to Colchis, and thus points far east to the origins of her mistress.[27] When Medea emerges to confront the chorus with her grievances, she brings attention to her foreignness:

"And a foreigner especially must adapt himself
[*chrê de xenon men karta proschôrein polei . . .*]."

[222]

When he learns of Medea's sorcery, her murders, Jason forgets about the benefits he had said she had gained from life among the civilized (536-54), and he accuses her of pure barbarism. She has passed for Greek; she too is counterfeit:

"There is no Greek woman who would have dared such
     deeds,
Out of all those whom I passed over and chose you
To marry instead, a bitter destructive match [*kêdos echthron
     olethrion t'emoi*].
A monster [*leainan*], not a woman, having a nature
Wilder [*agriôteran*] than that of Scylla in the Tuscan sea."

[1339-1343]

To Jason she appeared once as same, but must in this time of war among Greeks be recognized as other. She shares with her barbarian kin a tendency toward irrational dependence on truth-telling, expecting oaths to be kept and murdering when they are not. In another way, her reputation as a sorceress—her supposed ability to rejuvenate the old, to make fertile the childless, her horrible gift with *pharmaka*—is an extension of the barbarian character.[28] She is thought to be closer to nature, closer to her desires and to the world of natural poisons and remedies, like the mythical Centaurs.

This woman has other animal attributes. Unlike the heroic figures of Homeric simile, lions glorified in their courage and strength, Medea is seen as dangerously animal-like, as exhibiting unreason and violence which lower her, which make her inaccessible to the reasoning power of the chorus and of her articulate, sophistic husband Jason. She is impulsive and savage, like the bull and the lioness.

From the beginning the barbarian princess is seen as a potentially animal-like being. At line 92, the nurse calls her *tauromenên*, "becoming a bull." The difficulty of translating such a term into English reveals some of the compressive, allusive power of Greek—Medea is *bullified* in her anger. The nurse repeats her observation later:

"Such a look she will flash on her servants [*apotauroutai
    dmôsin*]
If any comes near with a message [*muthon*],
Like a lioness [*leainês*] guarding her cubs."

[187-189]

Language, *muthos*, that which distinguishes man from beast, has no effect on the heroine. In her last taunt at Jason, Medea accepts the denomination of her as a lioness:

"So now you may call me a monster [*leainan*], if you wish,
A Scylla housed in the caves of the Tuscan sea."

[1358-1359]

She is an animal, a hybrid woman, a monster created through metamorphosis.

All of Medea's characteristics mark her as "other," as different from her husband, the Greek male hero. The women of the audience, however, are drawn into her discourse by the speech in which she recounts the difficulties of every woman, the impossibility of divorce, the immobility of women in their homes, the pains of childbirth.[29] The role of the animal, barbarian, exile bride is the fate of every Greek woman. Within her adopted house each woman shares at times the frustrations and anger of Euripides' heroine.

By the very fact of her presence in the city, by her violence, her female, bestial, barbarian nature, Medea exemplifies the eruption of difference within the family, within the *polis*, among the Hellenes. Difference is represented by Euripides as *internal* rather than external, omnipresent in the body of the Greeks. The other, bestial, foreign, most of all female, is for Euripides a marginalized marked figure who is nonetheless at the center of the tragic drama. Her difference results from internal conflict, from forces within the *oikos* and the *polis* which do battle with one another.

The mode of reasoning by analogy persists; Medea as female is analogous to barbarian and animal. Yet the accumulation of force on the negative side of the polarities puts all into question. Jason—male, Greek, human—is set against Medea—female, barbarian, animal—and the city, as a culture, as a site for the reproduction of the family, is destroyed from within. By murdering her children, by murdering her husband's new wife, Medea brings an end to the line of Jason. The theme of reproduction and continuity introduced by Aigeus is thus pursued in the drama. The consequences of Medea's presence within the city are revealed as devastating to its future. The breaking down of language, of *tekmêria* (signs), is related to Thucydides' discussion of language and its perversion during the revolution in Corcyra (3.85.1). Signs which mark difference have become confused and contradictory; there is no clarity of intercourse among citizens. Revolution in the *polis*, between democrats and oligarchs, results in the same chaos as in war between Greeks, between men and women in the *oikos*.

Euripides offers, in the *Medea*, a continuous linear discourse about all the problems of difference, animal/human, Greek/barbarian, male/female. The single character Medea is marked in all ways as the other, the different, in the tragedy which bears her name. Unlike Aeschylus, who represented Hellene/Persian difference by showing forth only the barbarian, unlike Sophocles, who in the *Trachiniae* discussed human culture in terms of the excluded horse/man, Euripides represents all these figures at once in the person of his victorious heroine. The issue is no longer an alternate culture, like that of the Centaurs and Amazons, of the tribes described by Herodotos, of the Persians. Medea is not a whole other culture, but the other within the city, the female, the Spartan, the barbarian slave who comes to live inside the circle of the *polis* and who threatens to detonate violence which was previously seen as external to the Greek state. In the earlier tragedies the Persian threat looms, the violent culture of the Centaurs represents a threat to the wedding feast, to the Greek institution of marriage. In Euripides' play one of the partners of the marriage is herself an enemy, one who unlike Clytemnestra cannot be eliminated.

The Euripidean fashion of representing danger reiterates the formal structure of contemporary works of art, in that it expresses the presence of difference within the city, within culture. The earlier Heraklean metopes set the Greek hero at odds with creatures who lived at the edges of the world, to whom Herakles journeyed, like Jason in his search for the Golden Fleece. In later representations, especially those of the Amazons and Centaurs, these creatures invaded Greek culture, threatened to bring chaos into it, and were repulsed. On the frieze at Bassae, the allegorical figures of Centaurs and Amazons, anti-culture, anti-marriage, have penetrated the sacred space and threaten the closure of the *polis*. The presence of Apollo and Artemis on the frieze shows the hope of intervention from above, for *dei ex machina* to reorder and clarify difference. Like Artemis in the *Hippolytus*, the gods seem to offer a solution from outside. But in fact the gods too are implicated in the dissolution of categories posed by Euripides, to such an extent that a figure like the *Bacchae*'s Dionysos acts within the tragedy, using language as double-edged as Jason's to destroy the *polis* of Thebes.

In the *Bacchae*, Euripides' greatest masterpiece, the tragedian collapses all boundaries, fuses male and female, human being and animal, Greek and barbarian. Dionysus, who comes from the East, forces his seemingly barbarous worship on the women of the *polis*; the Hellenic Pentheus dies for his resistance to the invasion of Thebes. Dionysus is an androgynous being; the crisis of the tragedy is the moment when he convinces his antagonist Pentheus to dress as a woman and follow him to the mountain top. Dionysus has bestial qualities as well; he appears to Pentheus as a bull. Pentheus himself, torn apart by his mother, seems to her a lion cub.[30] The contradiction is not directly expressed as a battle within the house, between men and women, as it is in the *Medea*. In the *Bacchae*, Euripides brilliantly extends the collapsing of categories of difference to include even the physical space of the city. The tragedy ends after a devastatingly powerful, exhausting climax of destruction. The crisis of differentiation which is diagnosed in the *Medea* is realized apocalyptically in the *Bacchae*. The mother/son relationship ends in monstrous filicide, and the future of the *polis* is unthinkable.

The traditional marks of difference, excluding female, barbarian, animal from the city, no longer operate in Euripides' vision of the *polis*. The clichés that Jason utters about the life of justice and civilization among the Greeks, seem counterfeit, once we understand his purpose. He prefers civilized, muted, hidden violence; Medea prefers acts of blood. What is most revealing is Euripides' distance on these two solutions. Medea is pathetic at the beginning of the tragedy, Jason at the end. We trade civilized Greek brutality for the mysterious poisons and murder of the barbarian. Euripides sets Medea at one side of a polarizing dichotomy, the monstrous, alien, female side, and then refuses to valorize the human, Greek, male side at its expense. By bringing to life within the city and within the family this bestial, barbarian princess, Euripides tests all the categories of difference which contented Thales with his existence. He argues that difference cannot be excluded, that it has erupted inside, and that the city cannot survive on the old terms. Marks of polarity, the analogy of difference among barbarian, animal, female, are not trustworthy signs. Jason, the rational Greek male hero, is a teller of lies, a coward, a breaker of oaths; his language does not correspond to reality.

The Peloponnesian War, which set Greek against Greek in *polemos*, war, which was also *stasis*, civil war, precipitated the crisis of language, of categories of difference. It revealed the stresses, old and new, within the family of the Greeks.

Those comedies of Aristophanes in which women exert power, *Lysistrata*, the *Thesmophoriazusae*, and the *Ecclesiazusae*, also reveal an anxiety about male and female difference, about women's potential to disrupt the traditional patterns of order and exchange within the *polis*. In the comedian's representations,

women tend to use their power for the same narcissistic ends as
his male characters, with the exception of Lysistrata, who unites
the Hellenes in a joyous celebration of brotherhood in Eros.
Aristophanes' fantasy of peace records the degree to which the
war put strains on traditional categories. The comedy attempts a
fantastic solution, a unification of the Greeks as a people, without
an alien other, with the help of citizen women. Men alone were
seen as incapable of achieving an end to the war. Even such a
strange form of *polis* as a gynecocracy was conceivable for the
moment, if it could resolve the crisis. In *Lysistrata* the theme of
the Amazonomachy is evoked directly by the male chorus:

> "Or perhaps they fancy themselves as cavalry!
> That's fair enough: women know how to ride,
> they're good in the saddle. Just think of Mikôn's paintings,
> all those Amazons wrestling with men! No, it's time
> to bridle these wild mares!"[31]

>   [677-80]

The barbaric horse-women have indeed invaded the territory of
the *polis*, Lysistrata's troops have taken the Acropolis, and
threaten to reverse the tradition of men *on top*. Just as in
Euripides' *Medea*, the alien, woman, seems about to succeed in
dominating family and state. The sexual joke about women on
top is a measure of the need for radical solutions to the problems
of the Athenian state in its social and political crisis. The Amazons are no longer a danger; they represent, within the comedy,
an alternative to the destruction of internal war.

The Peloponnesian War clearly aggravated the social tensions
within Athens. The oligarchic revolution of 411 revealed the
difficulty citizens were having in sustaining a myth of democracy
in which all participated equally for the city's good. Slaves,
extreme oligarchs, democrats, even women were exposed as
separate entities within the *polis*. Differences were exaggerated,
and the old categories of definition were broken down. The mode
of speculation concerning difference, reasoning through polarity
and analogy, no longer described the divisions and breaks which
had erupted within. Euripides saw the irrational, the bestial, the
barbarian, the female, within the city and within the Greek hero

himself. Pentheus undergoes a metamorphosis before the eyes of the audience, becoming a female, becoming an animal, a lion cub who is the object of the hunt of his mother, turned barbarian by the god.[32] The tragedian reveals the inadequacy of the old logic of polarity. It is the project of the philosophers of the fourth century to discard that logic, to redefine difference, to replace the series of analogies which defined the *polis* as a community with a new logic, one of hierarchy, in which female, barbarian, and animal are set in relation to one another in terms of relative lack of and estrangement from *logos*.

I see both continuity and change in the "discursive formation" about difference in the fifth century B.C. Polarity and analogy remain the logical patterns most often employed throughout this period. The definition of man requires that a differentiation of kinds be established in terms of comparison. Thales defined himself as a Greek male human; difference is expressed in terms of the alien, the monstrous, the female. The "other" is seen as bestial, irrational, chaotic, subject to desire, hostile to marriage and exchange, enslaved. In tragedy, history, and in art, the description of these beings focuses on their common attributes. To know one such being excluded from the city is to know all such. Citizens share a common language, common institutions; those outside are often thought to be similarly allied in their difference. The attention of the citizen is frequently centered on what constitutes the city; the beings outside simply make up its boundaries. The fifth century citizen gazes at his equals, to understand the principles which unite him with other citizens. The barbarian, female, animal, are significant primarily in their contribution to that definition. The definition of the norm, the Greek male, thus depends in part on negation. Even Herodotos' descriptions of exotic foreign cultures served to define Greek institutions in their particularity as much as to offer insight into the lives of other kinds. His project adds to his listeners' and readers' understanding of what it means to be a Greek more than it illuminates the *kosmos* as a whole. The city knows itself better when it knows what lies outside the circle of equals. Myths, literature, and history all contribute to the project of the *polis'* coming to know itself. Centaurs, Amazons, and the barbarians, animals and females for whom they are emblematic, mark the boundaries of the self and the city, composed of equals. Analogy unites the citizens in their *isonomia*, they are in a relationship of polarized opposition to the "others," who are themselves linked in a pattern of analogy.

Yet, although the analogical model remains a constant in reasoning about race, species, and sexual difference, throughout this period, there are modifications in the uses of analogy which reveal eventually the ways in which it becomes unsatisfactory as a logical construct.

The elaborated pattern of polarity and analogy is flexible enough to accommodate the various historical moments between the Persian and Peloponnesian Wars, a period of relative peace, of the establishing of the Athenian Empire. By the end of the period, however, the logical model begins to break down. In the person of Medea the despised elements of the polarities are bound up together—she is barbarian, animal, woman. Her presence inside the city, as the wife of the human, Greek male, the hero Jason, marks the limits of the polarizing and analogizing model. The contradiction in the role of women—as the outsider within, the barbarian who is exchanged by the citizen in order to found the city—is made more apparent as the differences within Hellenic culture come to fruition. The Greeks can no longer sustain a description of themselves which makes identity rest on language, on one's common Hellenism, since within the body of the Hellenes there is division and war. The barbarian is within.

The *Medea*, one of Euripides' greatest works, is a brilliant examination of this contradictory position of women in the *polis*, the tragedy exposes the contradiction and reaches the most pessimistic of conclusions. Like the *Bacchae*, it represents barbarism inside the city, the contamination, through women, of culture which had thought itself invulnerable. Femaleness, barbarism and animality are rooted within culture, ready to explode and break the circle of community. The mode of reasoning through polarity and analogy cannot represent the complexities of relationship here; the fantasy of masculine *autarkeia* cannot be sustained. The Greek male is incapable of reproducing his culture without women, and his culture, throughout the waging of the

Peloponnesian War, is revealed to be broken and stratified throughout. Athenians fought with Spartans, Athenian slaves ran in great numbers to Decelea during the war, the fantasy of gynecocracy was played out in such texts as Aristophanes' *Lysistrata*, the Greek hero Alcibiades betrayed his own kind, the Athenians, to both the Spartans and the Persians.

In an important passage on *diaeresis*, division, in the *Politikos*, Plato points out that the division of mankind into Greek and barbarian is an error.

> It was very much as if, in undertaking to divide the human race [*anthrôpinon . . . genos*] into two parts, one should make the division as most people [*hoi polloi*] in this country do; they separate the Hellenic race from all the rest as one, and to all the other races, which are countless in number and have no relation in blood or language to one another, they give the single name "barbarian"; then, because of this single name, they think it is a single species [*genos*] . . . a better division, more truly classified and more equal, would be made by dividing . . . the human race into male and female. . . .[33]
>
> [262de]

His argument reveals the sense of division within, the inadequacy of polarization based on the old distinction of racial difference. His attempt to substitute sexual difference, however, as a valid criterion, is equally problematic, for the very contradiction described above, that women are both inside and outside culture. Plato's solution was rather to shift radically the terms of reasoning in response to the crisis of the fifth century. In the world Socrates knew, difference had entered the supposedly homogeneous culture of the city; new ways of reasoning about it required a break with the past and its antithetical, polarizing, analogizing, metaphorical logic.

NOTES

1.   On the working out of *isonomia*, see Hammond, op. cit., pp. 190, 204.

2.   See E. Lesky, *Die Zeugungs-und Vererbungslehren der Antike und ihr Nachwirken* (Weisbaden, 1951), on ancient theories of sexual difference.

3.   Parmenides' opposites included fire/night, bright/dark, sky/earth, hot/cold, dry/moist, rare/dense, light/heavy, right/left, soft/hard, and male/female; Pythagorean opposites were brightness/darkness, right/left, male/female. Guthrie, op. cit., vol. 2, pp. 77 and 245.

4.   See C.H. Emilie Haspels, *Attic Black-Figured Lekythoi* (Paris, 1936), and von Bothmer, op. cit., pp. 21 ff.

5.   Eleanor Irwin, *Colour Terms in Greek Poetry* (Toronto, 1974). See also K.J. Dover, *Greek Homosexuality* (Cambridge, Mass., 1978), pp. 68 ff.

6.   Irwin, op. cit., p. 111. She adds that evidence "suggests that *leukos* indicated not merely beauty in women, but another quality that was thought to be characteristic of them—their helplessness and need of protection" [121].

7.   Ibid. p. 111. For the source of these ideas about darkness and strength, see Onians, op. cit.

8.   Ibid., p. 129. See also Aristophanes' *Ecclesiazusae* 63-64, 385-7, 427-32.

9.   Gisela M.A. Richter, *ARV*, p. 39.

10.   Ashmole, op. cit., p. 191. He is speaking here of the mid-fourth century Mausoleum.

11.   Dover, op. cit., pp. 68-81.

12.   E.M. Blaiklock, *The Male Characters of Euripides* (Wellington, New Zealand, 1952), p. 21.

13.   The *Medea* was translated by Rex Warner.

14.   See Shell, op. cit., p. 96, on Oedipus as counterfeit.

15.   For the *Hippolytus*, see the superb edition by W.S. Barrett (Oxford, 1964). This translation is by David Grene. For similar sentiments, see Euripides' *Electra*, 373-379.

16.   The monetary metaphor suggests a parallel with the Athenian tetradrachm, which bore a *charactêr* of Athena crowned with a victory wreath, a sign of her defeat of the Persians. The mark itself was a lie, in a sense, after the city's defeat at the end of the

Peloponnesian War. On pictorial language in Euripides, see Shirley Barlow, *The Imagery of Euripides* (London, 1971).

17.   See N. Loraux, op. cit., pp. 43 ff.

18.   On the Pandora tradition, see Dora and Erwin Panofsky, *Pandora's Box; The Changing Aspects of a Mythical Symbol* (New York, 1962).

19.   Other fantasies included spontaneous generation of lesser beings from mud or slime. See *Antony and Cleopatra*, "Your serpent of Egypt is bred now of your mud by the action of your sun; so is your crocodile," says the learned Lepidus [2.7.27-38].

20.   *Mêdea* means genitals; the name of Euripides' heroine is variously etymologized— *mêdea* also means, "counsels, plans, arts" (LSJ).

21.   "Of all things which are living and can form a judgment
      We women are the most unfortunate creatures [*athliôtaton
            phuton*].
      Firstly, with an excess of wealth it is required
      For us to buy a husband and take for our bodies
      A master [*posin priasthai despotên te sômatos/labein*]; for not to
            take one is even worse.
      And now the question is serious whether we take
      A good or a bad one; for there is no easy escape
      For a woman, nor can she say no to her marriage.
      She arrives among new modes of behavior and manners,
      And needs prophetic power, unless she has learned at home,
      How best to manage him who shares her bed with her
      [*hotô malista chrêsetai suneunetê*].
      And if we work out all this well and carefully,
      And the husband lives with us and lightly bears his yoke
      [*mê bia pherôn zugon*],
      Then life is enviable. If not, I'd rather die.
      A man, when he's tired of the company in his home,
      Goes out of the house and puts an end to his boredom
      And turns to a friend or a companion of his own age.
      But we are forced to keep our eyes on one alone
      [*hêmin d'anagkê pros mian psuchan blepein*].
      What they say of us is that we have a peaceful [*akindunon*]
            time
      Living at home, while they do the fighting in war.
      How wrong they are! I would very much rather stand
      Three times in the front of battle than bear one child."
                                                        [230-251]

These last two lines reveal with special clarity the threat of masculinized women.

22. See W.K. Lacey, *The Family in Classical Greece* (London, 1968).

23. Ibid.

24. According to Vernant,

> ... on peut parler d'une coupure entre le mariage archaïque et celui que s'instaure dans le cadre d'une cité démocratique, à la fin du VIe siècle athénien. Dans l'Athènes post-clisthenienne les unions matrimoniales n'ont plus pour object d'établir des relations de puissance ou de services mutuels entre de grandes familles souveraines mais de perpetuer les maisons, les foyers domestiques que constituent la cité, c'est-à-dire d'assurer par la réglementation plus stricte du mariage la permanence de la cité elle-même, sa constante réproduction.

Vernant, "Le mariage," *Mythe et société,* pp. 62-63.

25. See the sensitive essay by B.M.W. Knox, "The *Medea* of Euripides," *YCS* 25 (1977): 193-225. On Euripides, see C.H. Whitman, *Euripides and the Full Circle of Myth* (Cambridge, Mass., 1974), T.B.L. Webster, *The Tragedies of Euripides* (London, 1967); P. Pucci, "Euripides: The Monument and the Sacrifice," *Arethusa* 10, 1 (1977), 165 ff.; and on The *Medea*, his sensitive, deconstructive reading of the play, *The Violence of Pity in Euripides' Medea* (Ithaca and London, 1980).

26. On women in Euripides, see the study by Philip Vellacott, *Ironic Drama, A Study of Euripides' Method and Meaning* (Cambridge, 1975), especially chapter 4, "Woman," pp. 82 ff., on Medea, pp. 106 ff. Vellacott argues that to call Euripides either a feminist or a misogynist is inaccurate. "He was a man who felt himself a member of the whole human race rather than of one half of it" [125].

27. Compare the beginning of the *Argonautica* of Apollonius Rhodius.

28. See Bacon, op. cit. On another of Jason's adventures, see Walter Burkert, "Jason, Hypsipyle and New Fire at Lemnos: A Study in Myth and Ritual," *CQ* n.s. 20 (1970): 1 ff.

29. On women's situation, see the summary of debate in Sarah Pomeroy, *Goddesses, Whores, Wives and Slaves: Women in Classical Antiquity* (New York, 1975).

30. On the *Bacchae*, see the excellent edition by E.R. Dodds, 2nd ed. (Oxford, 1960), and his *The Greeks and the Irrational,* René Girard, who builds his theory of the "mimetic double" on the play, op. cit.; and Charles Segal, "Euripides' *Bacchae:* Conflict and

Mediation," *Ramus* 6 (1977): 103-20, "The Menace of Dionysus: Sex Roles and Reversals in Euripides' *Bacchae*," *Arethusa* 11:1,2 (1978), 185-202, esp. 186-87, on Dionysus as the "dissolution and confusion of basic polarities."

31. Aristophanes, *Lysistrata*, an English version by Dudley Fitts (New York, 1954). On obscene reference to horses, see Henderson, op. cit., p. 165.

32. See Dodds, *Bacchae*, p. 224.

33. Plato, *The Statesman*, trans. by H.N. Fowler, with the *Philebus* and *Ion*, trans. W.R.M. Lamb, vol. 3 (London [Loeb], 1925).

VI
Hierarchy

The analogical model, typical of fifth-century speculation about difference—racial, sexual, species—defined the Greek male human in terms of a series of polarities which together articulated his nature. The others, that is, female, barbarian, and animal, were like spokes radiating from the hub of a wheel. At the center was the common element of each of the polarities, the center of the city and of culture, the graceful, civilized warrior of the classical frieze.

The Peloponnesian War wrought significant changes in the Greek city. Thucydides described the civil war of 427 in Corcyra in ominous terms:[1]

> To such excesses of savagery did the revolution go; [*houtôs ômê hê stasis proschôrêse*] and it seemed the more savage, because it was among the first that occurred; for afterwards practically the whole Hellenic world was convulsed, since in each state the leaders of the democratic factions were at variance with the oligarchs, the former seeking to bring in the Athenians, the latter the Lacedaemonians. . . .
>
> And so the cities began to be disturbed by revolutions, and those that fell into this state later, on hearing of what had been done before, carried to still more extravagant lengths the invention of new devices, both by the extreme ingenuity of their attacks and the monstrousness of their revenges. The ordinary acceptation of words in their relation to things was changed as men thought fit. Reckless audacity came to be regarded as courageous loyalty to party [*andreia*

philetairos], prudent hesitation as specious cowardice, moderation as a cloak for unmanly [*anandrou*] weakness. . . .
[3.82.1.3-4]

Language collapsed with the disintegration of the unity of the *polis*; with language went the old categories of differentiation of kinds.[2]

The chaos deplored by Thucydides continued in the fourth century, after the Spartans defeated the Athenians in war. The exchange of control, in revolutions within the cities, was accelerated to a dizzying pace, and the dominance over the whole of Hellas was traded among several cities. Thucydides' pessimism was justified. While Epaminondas led the Boeotians to victory, atrocities were committed by his people which he condemned. In 363 Theban exiles and some citizens of Orchomenos attempted to overthrow the Theban democracy, according to Diodorus (15.79.2), and the assembly of the Boetian League, discovering the plot, punished the Theban and Orchomenian anti-democratic conspirators by exacting *andrapodismos*—women and children were enslaved, the men killed, the city wiped out.[3] The violence and aggression once reserved for barbarians were continually enacted against fellow Hellenes.

The devastation brought about by continuing war brought social conflict, *stasis*. Hammond remarks that "During the fourth century there were larger numbers of slaves than ever before in most parts of the mainland . . ."[4] "In Greek states generally there was a sharp division between the interests of those who had property and those who had none, and it was the clash between them which led to revolution."[5]

When the labouring or wage-earning class contains a large number of slaves, the social gulf between those who own property and those who do not tends to widen. Wealth (*euporia*) and poverty (*aporia*) in the fourth century meant the possession or the lack of capital (*ousia*) rather than an ability to earn high or low wages. Even the smallest capitalist tended to look down on the wage-earning citizen who had to engage in a vulgar occupation (*banausia*).[6]

The growing dependence on slavery was a significant factor in the culture of the fourth century; it deepened the conflicts within the city brought about by endless dissension among the Greeks.[7]

M.M. Austin and P. Vidal-Naquet agree, in an analysis of the period called "the time of crisis":

> During the fourth century the gulf between rich and poor kept on widening. Egalitarian aspirations implicit in the notion of citizen aggravated tensions, and social inequalities were all the more keenly felt as a result.[8]

The myth of *isonomia*, of the city as a community bound together by sameness, could no longer be invoked in the definition of the human subject.

Artistic and literary production were affected by the changes in the life of the city. The great age of tragic drama ended with the death of Euripides—the period of civic architecture, the celebration of the city in works of art, ended as well. Monuments constructed in the fourth century were built more commonly in national shrines, or even in honor of individuals. The Mausoleum, built in Halicarnassus in 353 after the death of Mausolus, bore an Amazonomachy which was a celebration of the female warriors, spiritual sisters of Caria's two Artemisias.[9] The Amazons are no longer the enemies of the city; they are the ancestors of the Halicarnassian plutocrat who in 357 had helped Chios, Rhodes, and Kos to revolt from the Athenian Alliance.[10]

The shift in discourse discussed in the introduction occurs in the moment when the social conflicts of the fourth century are made explicit. The process of differentiation in terms of myth, polarity, and analogy, ceases to correspond to the needs of a changed world. In the fourth century, the most important texts were written for small groups of men, the elite citizens engaged in the project of philosophy. Much of Plato and Aristotle's discourse centers on problems of *stasis*, of civil war and conflict among people who would, in the fifth century, have thought themselves bound up in relations of similarity and community. Even legal texts, which give an extraordinarily vivid image of life in the fourth century, focus on conflict rather than on the resolutions of tragic drama which had celebrated community. Comedy changes, moving from an emphasis on the city and public life to conflicts within the family, between man and woman, between youth and age.

Some critics see, in this period, a broadening of the definition of the human, an extension of likeness to all men, and they point to the tendency in Greek thinking of the fifth century exemplified by such thinkers as Antiphon, who reputedly said:

> We revere and honour those born of noble fathers, but those who are not born of noble houses we neither revere nor honour. In this we are, in our relations with one another, like barbarians [bebarbarô(me)tha], since we are all by nature born the same in every way, both barbarians and Hellenes. And it is open to all men to observe the laws of nature, which are compulsory. Similarly all of these things can be acquired by all, and in none of these things is any of us distinguished as barbarian or Hellene. We all breathe into the air through mouth and nostrils, and we all eat with hands.[11]

As H.C. Baldry points out, this attempt to criticize class difference within the city is suppressed by most of the thinkers of the fourth century.[12] Where Baldry sees progress towards an appreciation of the common brotherhood of all men, I would trace within this expansion a growing appreciation of the utility of an explicitly formulated *hierarchy* within culture, and a gradually more explicit defense of differentiation through hierarchy in the fourth century.

Once Plato's project of *diaeresis*, of division and categorization, was explicitly acknowledged, the focus of discourse shifted away from reasoning through analogy, from the Greek/barbarian distinction, to internal divisions, towards a hierarchization which rationalized differences inside the troubled city.[13] Plato denied the utility of the Greek/barbarian polarity, turned his attention to male/female difference, but concentrated finally on reasoning based on subordination and dominance. Although he argues in the *Republic* (5469c, 470c) that Greeks should not enslave each other, and thus tacitly respects the traditional opposition, his argument is based on an idea of the city which articulates an *internal* division more important than that between Greek and alien.

Faced with conflict, with the disintegration of the traditional analogical model of differentiation, the philosophers of the fourth century did not extend their definition of the human subject to include all kinds. Instead, in an attempt to fix the form of the city in an unchanging, internally differentiated pattern, there evolved a new rationalization of social relations. Those relations comfortable to the elite of the city were attributed to natural qualities which were described in terms of a hierarchy of difference.

In the *Republic* Plato uses not analogy but a similar procedure, that of the extended metaphor, which he calls a myth, to set forth this hierarchization of kinds.[14] The myth of the metals is a sign of the "rupture," in Foucault's sense, the radical transformation of a discursive formation. In his *creation* of myth, Plato clearly goes beyond the thinkers of the fifth century, who reworked the myths inherited from the archaic past into literary and artistic artifacts. Yet Plato is also the link between reasoning through analogy and reasoning through a strict subordination of ideas. He still relies, especially for its persuasive quality, on the mode of analogy. The just city is analogous to the just man, and by examining the macrocosm, one understands the microcosm.[15] A synthetic myth is a model in miniature of how the just city might see itself.

In the myth of the metals in Book III of the *Republic*, Plato offers such a myth, an extended metaphor which projects a new articulation of difference within the city.[16] Socrates says if men were to believe his "Phoenician lie," the internal structure of the city would be secured. All men would be told they were children of a common mother, earth:

> While all of you in the city are brothers [*adelphoi*], we will say in our tale [*muthologountes*], yet God in fashioning those of you who are fitted to hold rule mingled [*xunemixen*] gold in their generation, for which reason they are the most precious—but in the helpers silver, and iron and brass in the farmers and other craftsmen.
>
> [*Republic* 3.415a]

Plato provides for some change, since at times a golden father would beget a silver son. Yet the analogy is made between kinds of men and kinds of metal, differences which are visible, essential, natural.[17]

Plato's new myth has the effect of shifting the temporal sequence in the Hesiodic myth of the races, also based on an analogy between men and metals, to a sequence in the present.[18] The hierarchy in Hesiod's version is temporal; his present race of iron represents a decadence in time from the golden age. In Plato's myth, the golden is now, but only in the superior class. Time does not alter the relationship among kinds of men; they remain fixed in an eternal hierarchy of value. Hesiod's myth of the metals led men to pessimism and resignation, since they were as a whole a race trapped in iron. Yet those living at one time were identical in their make-up. Plato's argument stresses not the nostalgia for a lost golden age, but rather resignation to a hierarchy of kinds in the present. His analogy, based on the metals, should shape men into an ideal relationship with each other within the city. They would not harm the earth, their common mother, nor would they struggle against one another in *stasis.*

The presentation of his argument in this oblique way, as a "lie," as a tale which would not be believed by the first generation of citizens, distances the author, mediates his speculation about difference and its effect on the audience. Thus it has elements of continuity with the mythic, analogical speculation of the fifth century concerning difference. Yet the myth of the metals breaks new ground in its attempt not to focus on the polarities which define the circle of the city by exclusion, but rather to look inside the city and reason about differences within. The analogical phrasing of the argument cannot be confused with earlier mythic expressions. Here begins the articulation of differences among the citizens themselves; the project of differentiation no longer rests on polarities and on simple analogy.

Plato's interest in hierarchy and internal differentiation is a sign of a rupture with the past, of new social conflicts that must be acknowledged in thinking about social life. Such internal stratification did of course exist in the fifth century; the legal structuring of the classical *polis* involved a spelling out, in terms of wealth, of distinctions on which magistracies, for example, depended. Yet the idea of hierarchy was not so prominent as a subject of discourse. The myth of the metals in the *Republic* is a crucial transitional text in the shift from analogical to logical thought about difference. The great chain of being is beginning to take the place of a circle with man at its center. There is an articulated, natural, eternal hierarchy even among citizens, who once were seen ideologically as identical parts of the culture of the *polis.*

Plato revised Hesiod's devolutionary myth.[19] Later, in the *Timaeus,* he recounted another myth which was related to the speculation of Empedocles cited earlier, concerning the process of species differentiation in time. His narrator's version of evolution here is similar to that spoken by Aristophanes in praise of Eros, in the *Symposium.* That myth projected change in time from a perfect spherical whole of original being to the divided yearning halves of the humans who now inhabit the earth. In another version of creation, in the *Timaeus,* the philosopher imagines a previous state from which the present is a severe decline.[20] Here too there is an elaborate version of a chain of being, of estrangement from the good:

> According to the probable account, all those creatures generated as men who proved themselves cowardly [*deiloi*] and spent their lives in wrong doing were transformed, at their second incarnation, into women.
>
> [90e-91a]

Women represent a decline, a punishment, a further estrangement from the happiness of the heavens.

> And he that has lived his appointed time well shall return again to his abode in his native star, and shall gain a life that is blessed and congenial; but whoso has failed [*sphaleis*] therein shall be changed into woman's nature at the second birth; and if in that shape, he still refraineth not from wickedness [*kakias*] he shall be changed every time, according to the nature of his wickedness, into some bestial form [*thêreion phusin*] after the similitude of his own nature. . . .
>
> [42bc]

In a graduated descent from one's native star, the soul moves down to birds, animals on foot, the footless and wriggling, to the status of fish and oysters, lower and lower on the scale of beings as they grow distant, in folly, from the heavens. This mythicizing version of evolutionary theory, although retaining some of the features of Empedocles' account, proceeds in the opposite direction from that of the earlier philosopher. Like Hesiod, Plato here envisions history as a descent from primordial unity.

More significant, however, is the hierarchical nature of the description. The philosopher maintains his closeness to the divine, moving upward in the scale of beings, while men who fail in the effort of philosophy are punished by becoming women in their second lives. No woman can be a philosopher; she must wait until after death, when her soul might be reincarnated in the body of a man. In a descending ladder of creation, Plato lays out the structure of the *kosmos*.[21] Just as in the myth of the metals, difference is defined in terms of relative value, and of progressive estrangement from the good. The Greek male citizen is no longer at the center surrounded by "others;" as the philosopher, he stands at the top of the chain of being, closest to the divine and to immortality. As the man of gold, the best, the *aristos*, he rules over all who live in the republic.

Plato begins the process of differentiation through subordination, while his ties to the model of reasoning of the fifth century, reasoning through polarity and analogy, are revealed even in passages explicitly concerning hierarchy and dominance of one kind over another. In a passage in the *Timaeus* describing the demiourgos' creation of the mortal body, the speaker employs the traditional analogies concerning female and animal, and elaborates a description of their nature in a way which illuminates the new rationalization of relations among kinds of beings:

> . . . since they scrupled to pollute [*miainein*] the divine (soul) . . . , they planted the mortal kind apart therefrom in another chamber of the body. . . . And inasmuch as one part thereof (of the soul) is better, and one worse, they built a division within the cavity of the thorax—as if to fence off two separate chambers, for men and for women [*diorizontes hoion gunaikôn, tên de andrôn chôris oikêsin*]—by placing the midriff between them as a screen.

[69d-70]

The male sex is assimilated to the divine part of the soul; men, like that divine soul, must be protected from the *miasma*, the pollution represented by women.[22] That worse part of the soul, likened to women, is superior to the worse of the body, which is like an animal:

> And all that part of the soul which is subject to appetites for goods and drinks, and all the other wants that are due to the nature of the body, they planted in the parts midway between the midriff and the boundary at the navel, fashioning as it were a manger [*phatnên*] in all this region for the feeding of the body, and there they tied up [*katedêsan*] this part of the soul which, though savage, [*hôs thremma agrion*] they must necessarily keep joined to the rest and feed, if the mortal stock [*genos*] were to exist at all.
>
> [70de]

Anger and appetite, bestiality and women, are metaphorically associated here, and to this extent the myth of Plato conforms to the analogical representation of the fifth century artists and poets, who conveyed ideas of difference through mythical juxtaposition, through the models of war and marriage. However, in another sense, Plato's description marks a radical shift from the earlier modes of reasoning. He is discussing subordination and hierarchy here: the divine principle, the divine soul, commands like a philosopher-king over his subjects, female and animal. His syntax, far more hypotactic than that of the poetic and prosaic texts of the fifth century, reveals the principle of subordination of elements. Even the elegance of Thucydides' prose is based on oppositions, on antithesis and parallelisms. The sentence cited above, from the *Timaeus*, reveals a more articulated subordination of elements, delaying the inferior part of the soul, the beastly, to last.

Composition in prose was in fact a more appropriate medium of expression for the thinkers of the fourth century in part because logical relationships needed to be communicated with greater subtlety, because relations of juxtaposition, opposition, contiguity, were not sufficient to encompass complexities of elaboration and subordination. The very difference which was seen at the end of the fifth century to have entered the democratic *polis*

had by the time of Plato entered the realm of the individual and
even of his body. Language was required to express new relationships of natural dominance and control, to describe explicitly the
crystalline totality of microcosmic and macrocosmic systems.

In the *Phaedrus*, for example, Plato has his characters discuss
the form of discourse in terms like those he uses concerning the
proper subordination of elements within the human body:

> But this, I think, is what you would affirm, at least, that
> every discourse [*logos*] should be constituted like a living
> being, having its own body [*sôma*], so as to be neither head-
> less nor footless, but having a middle as well as extremities,
> which have been written so as to be appropriate to each
> other and to the whole.
>
> [264c]

Every *logos*—that is, every argument, every rationalization, every
discourse—should be subject to the same type of subordination
and hierarchy, as well as organic connection, as the body described
at its moment of creation in the *Timaeus*.[23] In this elaborate and
hypotactic sentence, the impersonal verb *dein*, itself subject to
Phaedrus' speaking, *phanai*, controls the following elements of the
discourse, the *logos*. He moves from head to foot, from the mid-
dle to the extremities, and returns finally to the whole. The form
of the argument exemplifies the patterns of subordination and
control which it defends.

The notion of hierarchy can thus be seen to inform every
aspect of Platonic thinking, from the minute level of sentence
construction to his vision of the *kosmos* as a whole. Although his
manner of reasoning is analogical, in that he compares the
discourse to a body, the notion of hierarchy within the terms compared implies a relationship of hierarchy between those terms as
well. Thus, as the feet are subordinated to the head in the body,
so the body as a whole must be subordinated to the soul, and to
logos. The facts of subordination and hierarchy are universal.
Analogies may be made, but a chain of being can be constructed
which places all features of the universe in a graduated scale.

Gregory Vlastos' early work on the place of slavery in Plato's
thought clarifies the operation of metaphor in the Platonic text.[24]

Plato enunciates a new criterion for the discerning of difference, which is applied to order kinds within the microcosm of the body, and within the macrocosm of the universe as a whole. The metaphor becomes a vehicle not for expressing the analogous and common difference of animal, barbarian, and woman, from man, but rather of expressing various degrees of estrangement from the divine *nous*. Thus the relations of subordination and dominance are rationalized, seen as natural and proper.

> ... his views about slavery, state, man and the world, all illustrate a single hierarchic pattern; and ... the key to the pattern is in his idea of *logos* with all the implications of a dualist epistemology. The slave lacks *logos*: so does the multitude in the state, the body in the man, and material necessity in the universe ... Order is imposed on them by a benevolent superior: master, guardian, mind, demiurge ... the common title to authority is the possession of *logos*. In such an intellectual scheme, slavery is natural: in perfect harmony with one's notions about the nature of the world and of man.[25]

The metaphor of slavery grounds the Platonic scheme of differentiation. Slavery, a social fact, is the crucial model for relationships on all levels. The presence of slaves in the body of the state leads to a projection of enslavement everywhere; even the philosopher's prose style recapitulates slavery's relationships of subordination and hierarchization.

As Lovejoy pointed out, the great chain of being began with Plato. The inhabitants of the universe are set in a hierarchy of distance from the good by the philosopher. Each rung on the ladder is superior to that below it, and inferior to that above. The model of slavery, of domination, provides a way in which to see all "others" and to set them in a hierarchy. The fifth-century fantasy of Greek male *autarkeia*, revealed to be inadequate, as been replaced by the isolation of the idea, of *logos*, of that which made the citizen, the male, central within the democratic *polis*.[26] The philosopher, the best of those Greek male humans, set apart even from his fellow citizens by his golden nature, his proximity to the divine, is no longer at the center of human culture. He is rather at the top of the ladder, with all other kinds subordinated to the authority of *logos*. He is the living being least deprived of the power of reasoning.

The metaphorical centrality of the male has been exchanged for a reasoned justification of his superiority. Women, like slaves, like animals, are by their nature inferior; each is in varying degrees deprived of proximity to the divine. The fantastic creation myth of the *Timaeus*, which establishes the creation of various creatures in order, according to the behavior of the soul in its first incarnation, justifies the hierarchization of kinds in the present. Within the state, as within the body, appetite, anger, female, slave, animal, must be restrained and excluded from the places where decisions are made. Even the elaborate syntax of Plato, where main clauses rule the meaning, where subordinate clauses serve, mirrors the shift in ways of thinking. Difference does not make the others equal; subordination is relative and elaborately marked. Poetic, analogical uses of language are no longer appropriate to this project of philosophy, the rationalization of hierarchy.

Plato thus generalizes the metaphor of slavery to include all relationships. The social conflicts of the fourth century, the greater dependence on slavery, after a decline at the end of the Peloponnesian War, made his attempt to justify and rationalize the social relationships of the *polis* comprehensible. Difference had invaded and disrupted the city, and was acknowledged and almost despaired of by Euripides. Plato's response to the presence of difference was to look even more deeply inward and to justify the differences within the city in terms of an attribute of the citizen, *logos*. The Greek male human being thus reconstructed his notion of the world; the dominance of the citizen, the philosopher, was justified not in terms of *autarkeia*, but rather in terms of inevitable and natural superiority. The contradictory position of women, in which they were both objects of exchange necessary for the reproduction of the city, and outsiders, bestial and irrational, was also rationalized in a new way. Women were associated with the body, which was inferior to the mind; thus they, like the body, served the soul, the head, the philosopher, the male.

The description through metaphor of the great chain of being, a sign of Plato's continuity with patterns of thinking characteristic of the fifth century, was to a large extent abandoned by Aristotle. His language, even more prosaic and less imagistic than Plato's, clearly expressed a further rationalization of hierarchy. He focuses on the institution of slavery not as a metaphor for all relationships; rather, the idea of natural slavery provides a link in a clearly articulated chain of being, a link between man and animal.

Aristotle defined the continuum thus: "I call two things continuous when their respective boundaries, by which they are kept together in contact, become one and the same." (*Metaphysics* 10.1069a5).[27] As Lovejoy points out, this notion led to the search for the "missing link" in the eighteenth century; many thought they had found it in the brute Hottentot.[28] But Aristotle had long before established the slave as a kind of being mediating between man and animal:

> Therefore all men that differ as widely as the soul does from the body and the human being from the lower animal . . . these are by nature [*phusei*] slaves, for whom to be governed by this kind of authority is advantageous, inasmuch as it is advantageous to the subject things already mentioned. For he is by nature a slave who is capable of belonging to another (and that is why he does so belong), and who participates in reason [*logos*] so far as to apprehend it but not to possess it; for the animals other than man are subservient not to reason, by apprehending it, but to feelings [*pathêmasin*]. And also the usefulness of slaves diverges little from that of animals; bodily service for the necessities of life is forthcoming from both, from slaves and from domestic animals alike.[29]
>
> [*Politics*, 1254b15-25]

Robert Schlaifer, in an important essay, "Greek Theories of Slavery from Homer to Aristotle," calls the Aristotelian argument an "evasion."[30] He points to the difficulty thus:

This, then is the ultimate cause of Aristotle's chief error: he
tried to alter the common doctrine of slavery by making the
slave only a part of the master, and to make one man part of
another is, apparently, logically impossible.[31]

Nonetheless, the notion of natural slavery was a keystone in the
postulating of a continuum of living beings, one which Plato constructed in terms of a decline in the soul's status, as it underwent
metemphychosis.[32] Aristotle's argument, less mythical, is a
further rationalization of the reality of hierarchy, even though it
may be that, as Schlaifer remarks, "His only real concern is to
justify the existence in his ideal state of the class of slaves necessary for its proper functioning."[33]

The slave occupies, in Aristotle's vision, a place in between
man and animal, and there are other such mediate creatures.
Women too suffer from a natural deficiency, as the scientist
makes clear in his biological works:

Just as it sometimes happens that deformed offspring are
produced by deformed parents, and sometimes not, so the
offspring produced by a female are sometimes female, sometimes not, but male. The reason is that the female is as it
were a deformed male [*to gar thêlu hôsper arren esti
peprômenon*] and the menstrual discharge is semen, though in
an impure condition; *i.e.*, it lacks one constituent, and one
only, the principle of Soul.[34]

[*Generation of Animals*, 737a25-30]

Slaves are defined in terms of a lack; women too lack *logos.* They
are naturally, physically inferior to the male.

Thus the various kinds of beings which were once linked
analogously through their difference from the male are set in relations of absolute hierarchy. Interested in the *polis*, in *stasis* and
how to avoid it, Aristotle focuses more on the household and on
relationships within the city than on relations among different
states. The barbarian is dismissed as naturally more slavish
(*doulikôteroi*) than the Greek (*Pol.* 1285a20); Aristotle is more
concerned with the barbarian as a slave within a Greek household
than with the barbarians as enemies of the Greeks, and in fact

Aristotle's pupil, Alexander, tried to make all barbarians subordinate to him. In Aristotle's view, slaves and women are different from each other as well, except among the barbarians:

> Thus the female and the slave are by nature distinct [*phusei men oun diôristai to thêlu kai to doulon*] (for nature makes nothing as the cutlers make the Delphic knife, in a niggardly way, but one thing for one purpose . . .)
>
> [*Politics* 1252b]

Women are not the same as slaves, even though both kinds are inferior to men. What Lovejoy called "the principle of plenitude" is operating in the argument of the *Politics*. The universe is full, as well as continuous; there are no logical breaks in the scale of beings. Each kind is naturally superior, naturally inferior to those above and below it on the ladder.[35]

Aristotle, like Plato, is concerned to rationalize relations of hierarchy. He constructs, even more explicitly than Plato, a ladder of kinds of beings based on a theory of natural difference, of relative lack, which sets all creatures in a vertical hierarchy.[36] His understanding of the tripartite soul leads him to postulate full possession of it only in the male, the ruler of slave, women, children (1260a9-17).

Aristotle rejects the idea of "extreme" democracy, seeing it as a dangerous type of constitution, and prefers what he calls a mixed constitution, in which the people, the citizens as a whole, that is, male citizens, elect their magistrates from the higher classes of the city. He sees the ideal in a perpetuation of the oligarchical traditions of the "democracy," in which the most important offices of the state are maintained in the hands of the elite. This variety of constitution is preferable in part because it is the most stable, the least vulnerable to change. The whole of the *Politics* thus is based on the notion of the conservation of relations of dominance and submission. The male citizen, ruler in his home over women, slaves and children, participates alone in the governing of the *polis*, in this ideal state, and elects his superiors to positions of power within the city.

Aristotle argues for the universality of relations of hierarchy; difference, seen in terms of inferiority and superiority, is a natural phenomenon, as is slavery:

> Authority and subordination are conditions not only inevitable but also expedient; in some cases things are marked out from the moment of birth to rule or to be ruled. . . . because in every composite thing, where a plurality of parts, whether continuous or discrete, is combined to make a single common whole, there is always found a ruling and a subject factor, and this characteristic of living things is present in them as an outcome of the whole of nature. . . .
>
> [1254a25-30]

Difference is natural and internal to the family, to the state, to the universe of living beings. Men are superior to women, women superior to slaves, slaves superior to animals. The project of the fifth century, the differentiation of kinds of beings through simple analogy, has been abandoned for the rationalization of a rigid hierarchy of difference. Difference posed in terms of inclusion and exclusion, inside and outside, the city and the rest of the world, has been replaced by a strictly rationalized vertical system of differentiation, a new "dialectical motive."

In a significant passage Aristotle uses language reminiscent of Euripides' which reveals the extent to which fourth-century philosophy represents a rupture with the thinking of the fifth century. Aristotle is discussing the assertion that "man is by nature a political being":

> A man that is by nature and not merely by fortune citiless is either low on the scale of humanity or above it . . . [ho apolis dia phusin kai ou dia tuchên êtoi phaulos estin ê kreittôn ê anthrôpos . . .].
>
> [1253a5]

The citiless man is either closer to the animals, like a slave, or closer to the divine, like the wandering philosophers whose schools were to develop along with that of Aristotle.[37] All beings are set in hierarchy by Aristotle. Being without a city is not defined as being *outside* the polis; it is a particular situation, either worse or better than that of the citizen. Euripides' heroine Medea, on the other hand, uses the same term of herself:

"But I am deserted, a refugee, thought nothing of
By my husband—something he won in a foreign land.
[*egô d'erêmos apolis ous' hubrizomal/pros andros,*
ek gês barbarou lelêsmenê. . . .]"

[*Medea* 255-6]

Medea, by calling herself *apolis*, citiless, sets herself outside the community of the audience. She situates herself as a barbarian; her citilessness is analogous to her barbarian birth. She is far from home, and her barbarism, her violence, make her different, an element to be expelled, excluded from the city. *Apolis*, she is the wife, the barbarian, the lioness, the Centaur and the Amazon. Her a-polity is a geographical and psychological fact expressive of her otherness, of her difference from the audience she addresses. When Aristotle uses the term, he sets it in a hierarchy of value. A citiless man, in his view, is not invisible, absent from the discourse of the city. The citizen is the norm. Just as the woman is a deformed man, as the slave is a being between man and animal, so the citiless man is either stronger and better, or baser and weaker than the citizen. All kinds, barbarians, slaves, women, animals, are set in a scale of relative value throughout, not in terms of exclusion, of polarity, but rather in light of their deficiency, their relative deformation.

Aristotle, *the* philosopher, *the* scientist, for centuries to come, thus rationalizes the family and the state in a rigid hierarchy. The notion of natural difference, of a graduated superiority of kinds, with women, slaves and animals beneath the master citizen, justifies and attempts to eternalize the relations prevailing in the Greek world at the time of Aristotle. The Peloponnesian War revealed the inability of the old system of oppositions to guarantee internal stability. If, in the changed social and economic situation, the enemy was discovered within, a new rationalization of internal political control was necessary; the theory of natural hierarchy is that rationalization. To avoid *stasis*, one must acknowledge this hierarchy and order life accordingly.

Mind is superior to body; it must dominate the appetite even as the master must control wife, slaves, domestic beasts. Plato and Aristotle thus radically shifted the terms of the questioning of difference. From the analogical speculation about kinds of otherness which prevailed in the fifth century, they constructed, in a period of social and political crisis, a model of subordination, reflected even in genre and in prose style, which justified and rigidified the oligarchic relations of their world.

Offered as the description of *natural* differences, the great chain was the product of a particular moment of stress in Greek culture, when social conflicts within the city, the recognition of difference within, made it imperative that order be defined strictly in terms of mastery. The model of the slave, a being intermediate between animal and man, enabled the philosophers to imagine a society structured rigidly in terms of natural hierarchy. Their discourse, directed as a communication to an elite body of students, was ordered prosaically to reflect their ideas of subordination and mastery. It was restricted as a form to those possessing *logos.* Women and slaves were in principle excluded from discourse, silenced.

NOTES

1.   On this passage, see Lowell Edmunds, "Thucydides' Ethics as Reflected in the Description of Stasis (3.82-83)," *HSCP* 79 (1975): 73-92, and J.L. Creed, "Moral Values in the Age of Thucydides," *CQ* n.s. 23 (1973): 213-31. Edmunds demonstrates "the Spartan and oligarchic nature of Thucydides' ethical sympathies in this passage," and after comparing them to Hesiod's view of the Iron Age, shows that "Thucydides' ethical sympathies are not simply a matter of class feeling but reflect an archaic pattern of ethical thought" (74). On the authenticity of chapter 84, see Alexander Fuks, "Thucydides and the Stasis in Corcyra: Thuc., III, 82-3 versus (Thuc.), III, 84," *AJP* 92 (1971): 48-55.

2.   On the change in words' meanings as discussed here, see W. Wössner, *Die Synonomische Unterscheidung bei Thucydides und den politischen Rednern der Griechen* (Wurzburg, 1937), pp. 29-37.

3.   Hammond, op. cit., p. 506.

4.   Ibid., p. 524.

5. Ibid., p. 526.

6. Ibid. For the debate on the use of these categories for antiquity, see Moses Finley, *The Ancient Economy*, S.C. Humphreys, op. cit., and M.M. Austin and P. Vidal-Naquet *Economic and Social History of Ancient Greece, An Introduction*, trans. and rev. by M.M. Austin (London, 1977), pp. 3-28. The latter consider much economic history of antiquity to be framed in anachronistic terms; they append a bibliography on the controversy (pp. 28-29).

7. On slavery, see Finley, *Slavery*, Vogt, op. cit.; Rachel Sargent Robinson, *The Size of the Slave Population at Athens During the Fifth and Fourth Centuries Before Christ* (Greenwood, Connecticut, 1973).

8. Austin and Vidal-Naquet, op. cit., p. 139.

9. See Ashmole, op. cit., Chapter VI, "The Tomb of Mausolus," pp. 147 ff.

10. Hammond, op. cit., p. 515.

11. *Oxy. Pap.*, XI, n. 1364, fr. 2, Diels-Kranz 44B; English translation in Kathleen Freeman, *Ancilla to The Pre-Socratic Philosophers* (Cambridge, Mass., 1978), p. 148. On this fragment see, among others, F. Heinimann, *Nomos und Physis* (Basel, 1945), and E. Bignone, *Studi sul Pensiero Antico* (Rome, 1965).

12. Baldry, op. cit., pp. 59 ff.

13. I.M. Bocheński says Plato

> ... seems to have been the first to progress from a negative dialectic to the concept of positive proof; for him the aim of dialectic is not to refute the opinions of opponents but positive 'definition of the essence.'

A History of Formal Logic, trans. by Ivo Thomas (Notre Dame, Indiana, 1961), p. 35.

14. See Pierre-Maxime Schuhl, *Etudes sur la Fabulation platonicienne* (Paris, 1947), p. 99; L. Edelstein, "The Function of Myth in Plato's Philosophy," *JHI* 10 (1949): 463-81.

15. A. Olerud, *L'idée de macrocosmos et de microcosmos dans la Timée de Platon* (Uppsala, 1951).

16. Plato, *Republic*, with English trans. by P. Shorey, rev. ed. (Cambridge, Mass. and London [Loeb], 1937). Havelock describes Plato's procedure in the *Protagoras* and in *Republic 2* thus:

> Rather than attempting to convert evolution wholesale into devolution (as in the *Statesman* and *Laws*), he reproduces a copy of the scientific schematism but inserts Platonic additions and corrections in order to bring it into line with his own pre-suppositions. He edits rather than inverts his

source. He produces two speciously progressive accounts of man and of society, which however leave a final impression that progress is illusory and that it is vain to look for the source of morality in history.

[*Liberal Temper*, p. 87.]

For a summary of the debate on Plato's political theory, and its possible "authoritarian" tendencies, see Tobey, op. cit., pp. 49-51. See also Wood and Wood, op. cit., pp. 119-208.

17.   Aristotle cites this passage in the *Politics* [1264b10].

18.   See Robert Eisler, "Metallurgical Anthropology in Hesiod and Plato and the Date of a 'Phoenician Lie'," *Isis* 40 (1949): 108-12.

19.   See the important work by Ludwig Edelstein, *The Idea of Progress in Classical Antiquity* (Baltimore, 1967), especially pp. 102-18; D.R. Duff-Forbes, "The Regress Arguments in the *Republic*," *Mind* 77 (1968): 406-10; G.C. Nehrlich, "Regress Arguments in Plato," *Mind* 69 (1960): 88-90.

20.   Plato, *Timaeus*, with trans. by R.G. Bury (London [Loeb], 1929); on the *Timaeus*, see Paul Friedlander, *Plato*, vol. 3, *The Dialogues, Second and Third Periods*, trans by H. Meyerhoff (Princeton, 1969), pp. 355 ff. with bibliography, pp. 543-4.

21.   Luc Brisson discusses the appearance of the sexes in *Le même et l'autre dans la structure ontologigue du Timée de Platon* (Paris, 1974), ". . . la condition féminine, étant une déchéance, ne peut être imposée à la moitié des êtres humains avant même qu'ils n'aient eu le temps de meriter un tel châtiment" [456].

22.   See David Farrell Krell, "Female Parts in the *Timaeus*," *Arion* n.s. 213 (1975): pp. 400-21.

23.   Plato, *Phaedrus*, with Engl. trans. by H.N. Fowler (London [Loeb], 1917). See also Derrida's commentary on the *Phaedrus*, cited earlier.

24.   Gregory Vlastos, "Slavery in Plato's Thought," *Philos. Rev.* (1941), 289 ff., reprinted in Gregory Vlastos, *Platonic Studies* (Princeton, 1973), with a postscript written in 1959, in which he says, "I would not wish to suggest that slavery is *the* key to Plato's philosophy" [163].

25.   Ibid., pp. 161-2.

26.   On the wish for a world without women, see Solmsen, "Utopian Wishes and Schemes of Reform," chapter 3 of *Intellectual Experiments*.

27.   Aristotle, *Metaphysics*, with an English translation by H. Tredennick (Cambridge, Mass., and London [Loeb], 1935).

28. Lovejoy, *Great Chain*, 233-236, 255.

29. Aristotle, *Politics*, with an English trans. by H. Rackham (Cambridge, Mass. and London [Loeb], 1944).

30. Schlaifer, op. cit., p. 198.

31. Ibid., p. 195.

32. See also, on this question, S. Sambursky, *The Physical World of The Greeks*, trans. by Merton Dagut (London, 1963), especially chapter 6, "The World of the Continuum," on Stoic physics, pp. 132 ff.; and Alexandre Kojève, *Essai d'une histoire raisonnée de la philosophie paienne*, vol. 2, *Platon-Aristote* (Paris, 1972), pp. 332 ff.

33. Schlaifer, op. cit., p. 199.

34. Aristotle, *Generation of Animals*, with Eng. trans. by A.L. Peck, rev. ed. (Cambridge, Mass. and London [Loeb], 1953). See also 767b.

35. On Aristotle, see Havelock, *Liberal Temper*, pp. 295 ff.; Wood and Wood, op. cit., pp. 209-57.

36. For a full, idiosyncratic discussion of Aristotelian anthropology, see Stephen R.L. Clark, *Aristotle's Man: Speculations Upon Aristotelian Anthropology* (Oxford, 1975), especially pp. 107 ff., on slavery.

37. See Vernant's "Ambiguity and Reversal . . ." p. 492, for a discussion of this passage in relation to *Oedipus Rex.*

Conclusion

The invention of the new philosophical discourse in the fourth century B.C. meant not just the evolution of logical procedures for reasoning about the world. It involved the justification of a social order based on ideas of hierarchical difference, of the *natural* inferiority of women to men, of foreign slaves to citizens, of animals to slaves. The shift from analogical poetic discourse, and the abandonment of the artistic forms of the democratic *polis*—tragedy, old comedy, and monumental civic sculpture—were accompanied by a rupture in thinking about difference. Discourse in the fifth century centered on a definition of the Greek male citizen, the subject of *polis* culture. The thinkers and artists of the fifth century used a process of analogy to focus on their audience, the body of citizens who made up the city. Through a series of polarities, Greek/barbarian, male/female, human/animal, the culture centered on the Greek male human being who engaged in the civilizing institutions of marriage and its opposite, war.

The institutions of war and marriage were explored in the myths of Centaurs and the Amazons, figures from the archaic past who were seen as enemies of culture, who violated the patterns of exchange exemplified by marriage. Their violation of culture brought about *polemos*, war between differing kinds, between the Greek male human being and his bestial, barbarian, female enemies. The articulation of their opposition in works of art clarified the role of the citizen warrior, who was at the center of the city's discourse, who was the subject of the *logos*. The narrative structure of the *polis'* art represented the citizen male in various attitudes in relation to the "other"—fixed in static opposition on early classical metopes, set at the boundaries of the Parthenon, marking the limits of the city's ritual space, at last entering inside to invade the city's sacred territory.

Tragic drama participated in speculation about difference, in the project of defining the city and its citizens. The "others"—barbarian, Centaur, woman/barbarian/animal—were all represented in tragedy, shown in changing postures of resistance to the *polis* culture. Finally the contradictory position of women—as objects exchanged inside, as "others" outside—became visible at a moment when other polarities of definition were breaking down. Greeks were not a uniform kind of being, any more than barbarians, or women. At the end of the Peloponnesian War, the city could no longer sustain a definition of itself based on a series of polarities. Difference was recognized within the *polis*: *stasis* replaced *polemos*.

Difference in the fourth century was rationalized in terms of logical relationships which went beyond simple polarity and analogy. There was a new recognition of degrees of similarity and difference, and also of the necessity for grounding social relations more firmly, in this time of crisis, in supposedly natural attributes. Analogy was not abandoned, but the analogy of the master/slave relationship was given prominence and extrapolated to rationalize other relationships of subordination.

The philosophers extended the master/slave relationship, analogically, to all forms of connection. They broadened that model of relation to include every level of organization. Thus while they operated analogically, in a manner similar to that of the fifth-century thinkers, their model involved subordination at all levels to a higher order. The master was superior to his slave, but subordinate in another way to *nous*.

The rupture between a purely analogical and a hierarchical model occurred in large part because of the political and social crisis of the fourth century, because of the need to rationalize subordination in the face of a challenge. The unquestioned acceptance of slavery as a natural phenomenon, the dependence on the institution of slavery, led to a new discursive formation, a new way of understanding difference.

The great chain of being was created to justify the relationship of mastery. The Greek male citizen had dominated culture in the fifth century as well; his prominence was justified in the fourth century not in terms of absolute difference from other kinds, in terms of the dream of masculine self-sufficiency, but rather as a natural result of his proximity to the divine *nous*. The fact of his centrality, articulated in the fifth century, was overshadowed by a concern for the nature of hierarchy. The *polis* and its central actor had reached their limits, been defined and exploded from inside. Speculation now focused on relationships of power rather than on the particular subject of the *logos*. Reasoning ability, the possession of *logos* and judgement, became the criteria through which relative evaluation of kinds was made. Women were fixed as inferior to men, but superior to slaves, just as slaves were inferior to women, but superior to animals, just as animals were inferior to slaves but superior to inanimate tools.

Thus, the project of this philosophy, from its earliest expression in Plato and Aristotle, was from its beginnings centered on questions of hierarchy, of mind over body, man over women, "human" over foreigner, over slave. The model of dominance, with its concomitant dualism, as a description of natural relationships in all cases, survived as a defining structure in post-Platonic and post-Aristotelian discourse. The great chain of being fixed relations of superiority and dominance as a basis of philosophical intercourse. The conservative oligarchic thought of the fourth century philosophers was an ideal instrument for those in positions of power who followed them. The terms in which Plato articulated his problematic have defined Western philosophical discourse ever since. The prehistory of the great chain of being reveals another type of speculation about difference which was abandoned, in a rupture which celebrated *logos* in a new way, which made the deprivation of *logos* the criterion by which social relations of subordination and enslavement were articulated. Thus the great chain of being had many "curiously" unhappy consequences in the history of Western thought: the celebration of the philosopher, the master, the male; the subordination of the body, the female, the slave to this being at the top of the ladder of existence.

Index

Achelôös, 97, 99, 102
Achilles, 29, 33, 69
acropolis, 33, 121
Aeschylus, 7, 8, 47 n.58, 55, 90;
    difference, 80-92, 112, 118;
    Oresteia, 63, 91; *Persae*, 16-17,
    54, 80-92, 95, 96, 110; polariz-
    ing logic, 80-92; *Seven Against
    Thebes*, 91; *Suppliants*, 47 n.58,
    82; visionary mind, 17
Aetius, 69
Agave, 119-120
agôn: Greek/barbarian, 60, 61, 62,
    82, 90, 95; Herakles, 57-58, 97,
    103, 119; human/animal, 60, 61,
    82; marriage, 88; male/female,
    61; on metope, 57-58, 59, 60,
    63, 75 n.47, 80, 89, 95, 96, 97,
    102, 106, 110, 116, 119; *polis*,
    60, 65-66, 104-05, 119, 132,
    134, 142, 145, 151; in tragedy,
    80-81, 82, 89, 104-05, 116
agora, 79, 110
Alcibiades, 109 n.17, 124
Alexander, 2, 19 n.8, 90, 143
Amazonomachy, 49-71; Areo-
    pagus, 33, 47 n.58; Centau-
    romachy, 49-50, 53, 55-57, 61,
    62, 64-65, 67, 70, 103, 112; at
    Delphi, 51, 57, 58-59, 60, 66;
    Geryonomachy, 50, 51, 57;
    Lysistrata, 99, 120-21, 125; Mau-
    soleum, 131; Parthenon, 61,
    62-64, 103; Persians, 54-57, 61,
    64, 67, 82; popularity, 53-54;
    shield of Athena, 63-64; Stoa

Poikile, 35, 54, 56; temple of
    Apollo, 64-66, 112; Themiskyra,
    58, 60, 61-62, 65; Theseion, 35,
    61; vase painting, 34, 35, 50-51,
    59, 61, 65, 111
Amazons, 25-42, 47 n.58;
    Achilles, 33, 69; appearance, 35,
    54, 111; in Athens, 33, 40, 54,
    58, 59, 62, 64, 66, 71, 121; Bel-
    lerophon, 32-33; boundaries, 27,
    37, 39, 41, 59, 63, 70, 96, 111,
    123; Centaurs, 27, 32, 34, 39,
    40, 42, 49-50, 53, 54-57, 62, 63,
    65, 67, 68, 70, 96, 110; chaste,
    34; before difference, 34;
    exchange, 40, 42, 56, 68, 70;
    Geryon, 50-51, 57, 58, 60, 61,
    65; girdle of Hippolyta, 33, 40,
    58; gods, 34; Herakles, 32, 33,
    34, 35, 40, 50-51, 57-58, 59, 65,
    66, 74 n.37; Hippolyta, 33, 40,
    58; horse-women, 34; *Iliad*, 33;
    Lysistrata, 99, 121, 124; mar-
    riage, 34, 36, 39, 40, 42, 68, 70,
    150; men, 34, 40, 70, 110;
    Penthesileia, 33; Persians, 54-57,
    61, 64, 67, 71, 96; Sauromatae,
    36-37; Scythian men, 34; sexual-
    ity, 34, 35, 65, 70, 111;
    Theseus, 32, 33, 40, 51, 54, 56,
    57-58, 59, 60, 65, 66; tempera-
    ment, 34, 51, 55, 56, 65, 70; as
    warriors, 34, 35, 54, 64-65, 70
analogy: in architecture, 51, 56,
    58, 63-65, 70, 71; definition, 3,
    19 n.9, 51; defines other, 42,

153